D0988628

PSALMS 1–72

Richard J. Clifford, S.J.

COLLEGEVILLE BIBLE COMMENTARY

THE LITURGICAL PRESS

Collegeville, Minnesota

ABBREVIATIONS

Gen—Genesis
Exod—Exodus
Lev—Leviticus
Num—Numbers
Deut—Deuteronomy
Josh—Joshua
Judg—Judges
Ruth—Ruth
1 Sam—1 Samuel
2 Sam—2 Samuel
1 Kgs—1 Kings
2 Kgs—2 Kings
1 Chr—1 Chronicles
2 Chr—2 Chronicles
Ezra—Ezra
Neh—Nehemiah
Tob—Tobit
Jdt—Judith
Esth—Esther
1 Macc—1 Maccabees
2 Macc—2 Maccabees
Job—Job
Ps(s)—Psalms(s)
Prov—Proverbs

Eccl—Ecclesiastes
Song—Song of Songs
Wis—Wisdom
Sir—Sirach
Isa—Isaiah
Jer—Jeremiah
Lam—Lamentations
Bar—Baruch
Ezek—Ezekiel
Dan—Daniel
Hos—Hosea
Joel—Joel
Amos—Amos
Obad—Obadiah
Jonah—Jonah
Mic—Micah
Nah—Nahum
Hab—Habakkuk
Zeph—Zephaniah
Hag—Haggai
Zech—Zechariah
Mal—Malachi
Matt—Matthew
Mark—Mark
Luke—Luke

John—John
Acts—Acts
Rom—Romans
1 Cor—1 Corinthians
2 Cor—2 Corinthians
Gal—Galatians
Eph—Ephesians
Phil—Philippians
Col—Colossians
1 Thess—1 Thessalonians
2 Thess—2 Thessalonians
1 Tim—1 Timothy
2 Tim—2 Timothy
Titus—Titus
Phlm—Philemon
Heb—Hebrews
Jas—James
1 Pet—1Peter
2 Pet—2 Peter
1 John—1 John
2 John—2 John
3 John—3 John
Jude—Jude
Rev—Revelation

Nihil obstat: Robert C. Harren, J.C.L., *Censor deputatus.*

Imprimatur: ✢ George H. Speltz, D.D., Bishop of St. Cloud. June 5, 1986.

ISBN 0-8146-1479-5 (volume 22 O.T.); ISBN 0-8146-1394-2 (complete set O.T.)

Library of Congress Cataloging-in-Publication Data

Clifford, Richard J.

    Psalms 1–72.

    (Collegeville Bible commentary. Old Testament ; 22)

    1. Bible. O.T. Psalms I–LXXII—Commentaries.
I. Bible. O.T. Psalms I–LXXII. English. New
American Bible. 1986. II. Title. III. Title: Psalms
one-seventy-two. IV. Title: Psalms one through seventy-two. V. Series.
BS1430.3.C55 1986   223′.2077   86-21027
ISBN 0-8146-1479-5

Cover: "The Lord is my shepherd; I shall not want. In verdant pastures he gives me repose" (Ps 23:1-2). *Photo: Flock of sheep at Nazareth, by Placid Stuckenschneider, O.S.B.*

CONTENTS

The Book of Psalms

Introduction

At the center of every psalm is the presence of Yahweh, the God of Israel, "the Lord" in Jewish and Christian translations. Yahweh is present to the psalmists most often in the temple. Built on Mount Zion in Jerusalem by King Solomon in the tenth century B.C.E. and rebuilt in the late sixth century B.C.E., after the Babylonian Exile, the temple complex was the site of the three great annual festivals: Passover in early spring, Pentecost seven weeks later, and Ingathering (also called the Feast, or Booths) in early fall. In the temple court the people encountered their Lord; they recalled the moment of their creation, the Exodus-Conquest (sometimes depicted in mythic language of victory over the sea) in solemn liturgical remembering.

According to the psalms, the temple was not the only institution through which Yahweh was present to the people. They also encountered God in the king, son of God by adoption, intermediary between God and people, and conduit of divine blessings to the people. Another mode of presence was the divine word to Israel, the law or *torah*. The Christian church sees in Jesus Christ and in the church that embodies him a presence so definitive as to include and fulfill all previous modes of presence.

The 150 psalms express Israel's experience of the Holy One, directly and concretely, with a wide range of feeling. As deep and as true as the psalmists' feelings are, their expression is strongly marked by the ancient Near Eastern tradition of hymnody. Genuine religious feeling, a strong tradition, and literary craft—these made the psalms. To know them, to share their religious feeling, one must be willing to study the tradition and the craft.

The most concise approach to the tradition and craft of the psalms is that perfected by Hermann Gunkel (1862–1932), professor of Bible at Berlin and later at Halle, in his great commentary (1926) and in his introduction (1933). Gunkel, with a romantic's love of the popular feeling and spontaneity of the psalms, and with a scholar's mastery of the relevant literatures and languages, recognized that the thoughts and emotions of the psalms are expressed in extremely traditional ways, "forms" or "genres," customary ways of speaking in the ancient Near East. Largely on the basis of his observations, scholars divide the psalms into a relatively few genres or forms: *laments* (individual or communal), *thanksgivings* (individual or communal), and *hymns*. A few psalms do not come directly under the above categories; these include royal psalms, songs of Zion, songs of trust, and psalms influenced by wisdom literature themes. These are classed according to their subject matter rather than according to their formal structure.

We sketch below the typical features of the main genres of (A) lament, (B) thanksgiving, and (C) hymn. References to this general treatment will be given throughout the commentary.

A. Psalms of **lament** are characterized by:

—a direct, unadorned cry to Yahweh.

—Complaint. A vivid description of the affliction of the community, such as military or agricultural distress, or of the individual, such as sickness, unfair legal process, treachery of former friends, or the consequences of sin. Sometimes there is a protestation of innocence; the punishment is undeserved.

—Expression of trust. Despite the crisis, the psalmist maintains a hope, however modest, that God will act. Such a hope is often introduced by "but" or "nevertheless."

—Petition. The psalmist prays for his own or his people's rescue, and often for the enemies' downfall.

—Words of assurance. A word delivered to the psalmist by a priest in the course of the lament. Only rarely is it transmitted with the text of the psalm, for example, Pss 15:5 and 60:6-8. Apparently, it was considered the priest's part, not the petitioner's.

—Statement of praise. A serene statement at the end of the psalm, in striking contrast to the anxiety of what has gone before. The psalmist states the intention to live the word of assurance delivered by the priest *as the word of the Lord.*

Each lament records a drama with three actors: the psalmist, God, and "the wicked." In the complaint the psalmist dramatizes his plight and protests his innocence so as to move God to action: Will you, just God, allow this innocent poor person to be vanquished by the wicked? In community laments the question is: Will you allow your choosing of Israel to be nullified by another power? The words of assurance, the fifth element in the outline above, function like a judicial verdict, affirming that the Lord does not allow evil to triumph ultimately and will vindicate the poor person. In the vow of praise the psalmist promises to live in the hope that God will act.

B. **Thanksgiving psalms** are closely allied to laments; in essence they are the report of rescue from the hands of the wicked. The term "thanksgiving" is somewhat misleading, for in the Bible to "give thanks" does not mean to say "thank you" but to tell publicly of the rescue that has occurred. The audience then recognizes the hand of Yahweh and gives praise. As a result, Yahweh's glory is acknowledged by human beings.

Most such psalms begin with an expression of thanks and then describe the act of rescue: the psalmist was in distress, even near despair, cried to Yahweh for help, and was saved. The psalmist is conscious of the congregation as he delivers his prayerful report, for the world must acknowledge what Yahweh has done.

C. The **hymn** is simple in its structure: a call to worship, often with the addressees named; for example, "Praise the Lord, all you nations," (Ps 117:1). The main section gives the basis for praise and is introduced by "for." The basis for praise is the activity that displays the Lord's majesty on earth.

The Psalter is an anthology of small collections finally edited into five books, perhaps in imitation of the five books of the Pentateuch: Psalms 1–41, 42–72, 73–89, 90–106, and 107–150. It is sometimes called the hymnbook of the second temple of 515 B.C.E.–A.D. 70, an accurate designation as long as we remember that songs of many periods of Israel's history, including the pre-exilic, are represented in the collection, and that non-liturgical considerations may have influenced the later editing.

A striking feature of the later editing of the Psalter is the superscription, like that written at the beginning of Psalm 51: "A psalm of David, when Nathan the prophet came to him after his sin with Bathsheba" (see 1 Sam 12). Such redactional statements make psalms originally at home in the temple liturgy applicable to any individual, since David was the typical Israelite; what happened to him could happen to each of us.

The Book of Psalms

Text and Commentary

PSALM 1

True Happiness

I

¹Happy the man who follows not
the counsel of the wicked
Nor walks in the way of sinners,
nor sits in the company of the inso-
lent,
²But delights in the law of the LORD
and meditates on his law day and
night.

³He is like a tree
planted near running water,
That yields its fruit in due season,
and whose leaves never fade.
[Whatever he does, prospers.]

II

⁴Not so the wicked, not so;
they are like chaff which the wind
drives away.
⁵Therefore in judgment the wicked shall
not stand,
nor shall sinners, in the assembly of
the just.

BOOK I: PSALMS 1–41

Psalm 1

This poem is classified as a wisdom psalm because it depicts and contrasts dramatically the "two ways," the two fundamental options for human
beings. Hebrew rhetoric often views moral life as action, as choosing, and
describes it by mentioning typical actions and their consequences. The psalm
divides people into two groups: those obedient to the will of the Lord in verses
1-3, and the wickedly disobedient in verses 4-5. Each group will experience
the consequences of their activity: life and prosperity for the obedient, ostracism and unrootedness for the wicked. The psalmist is not self-righteous,
disdainfully separating people into righteous and sinners; rather, he celebrates
the Lord's world, which is experienced as inherently just, rewarding the righteous and punishing the unrighteous. One places oneself in the community
of the righteous or of the unrighteous by one's actions. The psalm therefore
invites the person of faith to join those who revere and obey the Lord and
to avoid those who rebel against the Lord.

⁶For the LORD watches over the way of
 the just,
 but the way of the wicked vanishes.

PSALM 2

The Universal Reign of the Messiah

I

¹Why do the nations rage
 and the peoples utter folly?
²The kings of the earth rise up,
 and the princes conspire together
 against the LORD and against his
  anointed:
³"Let us break their fetters
 and cast their bonds from us!"

II

⁴He who is throned in heaven laughs;
 the LORD derides them.
⁵Then in anger he speaks to them;
 he terrifies them in his wrath:
⁶"I myself have set up my king
 on Zion, my holy mountain."

III

⁷I will proclaim the decree of the LORD:
 The LORD said to me, "You are my
  son;

this day I have begotten you.
⁸Ask of me and I will give you
 the nations for an inheritance
 and the ends of the earth for your
  possession.
⁹You shall rule them with an iron rod;
 you shall shatter them like an earthen
  dish."

IV

¹⁰And now, O kings, give heed;
 take warning, you rulers of the earth.
¹¹Serve the LORD with fear, and rejoice
 before him;
 with trembling ¹²pay homage to him,
Lest he be angry and you perish from
 the way,
 when his anger blazes suddenly.
 Happy are all who take refuge in him!

PSALM 3

Trust in God in Time of Danger

¹A psalm of David, when he fled from his son
Absalom.

I

²O LORD, how many are my adversaries!
 Many rise up against me!

Psalm 2

  This royal psalm affirms the Israelite king to be regent of the Lord. In
four sections of approximately equal length (vv. 1-3, 4-6, 7-9, 10-11), the
Lord's sovereignty over the earth, a sovereignty exercised by the Israelite
king, is expressed in a series of actions. In verses 1-3 the kings of the world
try to throw off the dominion of the Lord and the Lord's anointed: "Let us
break their fetters!" Such a wish is laughable (vv. 4-6). There is but one God
in the heavens; the "gods" that the nations believe guide their destinies are
not powerful before the one God who chose Israel. In verses 7-8 the narra-
tor pronounces, in the legal adoption language of the day, the divine decree
that has made the Israelite king the representative on earth of the one true
God. In principle, then, this king is the ruler of the whole world and all its
other kings (vv. 8-9). In verses 10-11 the unruly kings are warned: Revere
the Lord, revere the king!

Psalm 3

  In this lament (A—see p. 6) the psalmist is surrounded by enemies who
threaten his life and deny the possibility that the Lord will come to the res-

³Many are saying of me,
  "There is no salvation for him in
    God."
⁴But you, O LORD, are my shield;
  my glory, you lift up my head!

II

⁵When I call out to the LORD,
  he answers me from his holy moun-
    tain.
⁶When I lie down in sleep,
  I wake again, for the LORD sustains
    me.
⁷I fear not the myriads of people
  arrayed against me on every side.

III

⁸Rise up, O LORD!
  Save me, my God!
For you strike all my enemies on the
    cheek;
  the teeth of the wicked you break.
⁹Salvation is the LORD's!
  Upon your people be your blessing!

PSALM 4
Joyful Confidence in God

¹For the leader; with stringed instruments. A psalm
of David.

I

²When I call, answer me, O my just God,
  you who relieve me when I am in
    distress;
  Have pity on me, and hear my
    prayer!

II

³Men of rank, how long will you be dull
    of heart?
  Why do you love what is vain and
    seek after falsehood?
⁴Know that the LORD does wonders for
    his faithful one;
  the LORD will hear me when I call
    upon him.
⁵Tremble, and sin not;
  reflect, upon your beds, in silence.
⁶Offer just sacrifices,
  and trust in the LORD.

III

⁷Many say, "Oh, that we might see better
    times!"
  O LORD, let the light of your counte-
    nance shine upon us!
⁸You put gladness into my heart,
  more than when grain and wine
    abound.
⁹As soon as I lie down, I fall peacefully
    asleep,

cue (vv. 2-3). Against such taunts, the psalmist hopes that the Lord will answer heartfelt prayer, even managing to boast that the Lord will give
protection in life's most vulnerable moment—lying down to sleep (vv. 5-7).
Verse 8 prays that the Lord, like a warrior, will defang the taunting enemy.
Such defeat of the enemy constitutes public vindication of the psalmist. Verse
9 is a peaceful statement of praise uttered after hearing the oracle of salvation promising rescue. The "salvation," or rescue, that the enemies denied
will come without fail.

Psalm 4
This lament shows a more vigorous confidence in the Lord's protection
of the just than in most instances of the genre; it can be called a song of
trust. The psalmist prays to the God whose help was experienced in the past
(v. 2). Out of that confidence he lectures the wicked; they, not he, are in
danger and should make their peace with the Lord through ritual means.

for you alone, O LORD,
  bring security to my dwelling.

PSALM 5
Prayer for Divine Help

[1]For the leader; with wind instruments. A psalm of David.

I

[2]Hearken to my words, O LORD,
  attend to my sighing.
[3]Heed my call for help,
  my king and my God!
 To you I pray, [4]O LORD;
  at dawn you hear my voice;
  at dawn I bring my plea expectantly
    before you.

II

[5]For you, O God, delight not in wickedness;
  no evil man remains with you;
[6] the arrogant may not stand in your sight.
 You hate all evildoers;
[7] you destroy all who speak falsehood;
 The bloodthirsty and the deceitful
  the LORD abhors.

III

[8]But I, because of your abundant kindness,
  will enter your house;
 I will worship at your holy temple
  in fear of you, [9]O LORD;
 Because of my enemies, guide me in
    your justice;
  make straight your way before me.

IV

[10]For in their mouth there is no sincerity;
  their heart teems with treacheries.
 Their throat is an open grave;
  they flatter with their tongue.
[11]Punish them, O God;
  let them fall by their own devices;
 For their many sins, cast them out
  because they have rebelled against
    you.

V

[12]But let all who take refuge in you
  be glad and exult forever.
 Protect them, that you may be the joy
  of those who love your name.
[13]For you, O LORD, bless the just man;
  you surround him with the shield of
    your good will.

The psalmist's nearness to God enables him to warn those who have distanced themselves to be reconciled (vv. 3-6). That nearness also makes the psalmist a model of the blessings of God (vv. 7-9).

Psalm 5

In this lament (A) the psalmist contrasts the security of the house of the Lord (vv. 8-9 and 12-13) with the danger of the company of the wicked (vv. 5-7 and 10-11). He therefore prays insistently for God to hear him (vv. 2-4). Both worlds—the danger of the wicked and the enjoyment of the righteous—are imagined concretely: verses 8-9 describe admittance to the temple; in verses 12-13 the verbs "be glad," "exult," and "be the joy of" describe the singing and shouting of liturgical procession.

Psalm 6

This lament (A) is one of the Penitential Psalms, a designation that originated in the seventh century A.D. for seven psalms (6, 32, 38, 51, 102, 130, 143) that are especially suitable to express repentance. The psalmist feels

PSALM 6
Prayer in Time of Distress

[1]For the leader; with stringed instruments, "upon the eighth." A psalm of David.

I

[2]O Lord, reprove me not in your anger,
  nor chastise me in your wrath.
[3]Have pity on me, O Lord, for I am languishing;
  heal me, O Lord, for my body is in terror;
[4]My soul, too, is utterly terrified;
  but you, O Lord, how long . . . ?

II

[5]Return, O Lord, save my life;
  rescue me because of your kindness,
[6]For among the dead no one remembers you;
  in the nether world who gives you thanks?

III

[7]I am wearied with sighing;
  every night I flood my bed with weeping;
  I drench my couch with my tears.

[8]My eyes are dimmed with sorrow;
  they have aged because of all my foes.

IV

[9]Depart from me, all evildoers,
  for the Lord has heard the sound of my weeping;
[10]The Lord has heard my plea;
  the Lord has accepted my prayer.
[11]All my enemies shall be put to shame in utter terror;
  they shall fall back in sudden shame.

PSALM 7
An Appeal to the Divine Judge

[1]A plaintive song of David, which he sang to the Lord because of Cush the Benjaminite.

I

[2]O Lord, my God, in you I take refuge;
  save me from all my pursuers and rescue me.
[3]Lest I become like the lion's prey,
  to be torn to pieces, with no one to rescue me.

II

[4]O Lord, my God, if I am at fault in this,

burdened with the consequences of his sin—bodily and mental distress (vv. 3, 7-8) and harassment by enemies (vv. 9, 11). The word "sin" in the Bible can denote not only the act of sinning but its consequences as well. Sin brought consequences that had to be borne, consequences such as personal distress and the taunts of enemies. The speaker pleads for forgiveness not only for the past act of sin but also for the consequences of that act. Thus he asks that his bodily self be healed and that his enemies depart. The return of health and the departure of enemies publicly demonstrate divine acceptance. In the last stanza the psalmist shows the effect of hearing the word of assurance—confidence in the Lord's nearness.

Psalm 7

Psalm 7 is a lament (A), specifically the prayer of an accused person who flees to the presence of the Lord in the sanctuary for justice and protection (vv. 2-3). He takes an oath that he is innocent of any crime that would justify his enemies' attack (vv. 4-6). Since in this case he is innocent, having allowed God to scrutinize his inmost heart, the attacks upon him constitute attacks upon the innocent just person. The God of justice must therefore put

if there is guilt on my hands,
⁵If I have repaid my friend with evil,
I who spared those who without
cause were my foes—
⁶Let the enemy pursue and overtake me;
let him trample my life to the ground,
and lay my glory in the dust.

III
⁷Rise up, O Lord, in your anger;
rise against the fury of my foes;
wake to the judgment you have decreed.
⁸Let the assembly of the peoples surround you;
above them on high be enthroned.
⁹ [The Lord judges the nations.]
Do me justice, O Lord, because I am just,
and because of the innocence that is mine.
¹⁰Let the malice of the wicked come to an end,
but sustain the just,
O searcher of heart and soul, O just God.

IV
¹¹A shield before me is God,
who saves the upright of heart;
¹²A just judge is God,
a God who punishes day by day.
¹³Unless they be converted, God will sharpen his sword;
he will bend and aim his bow,

¹⁴Prepare his deadly weapons against them,
and use fiery darts for arrows.

V
¹⁵He who conceived iniquity and was pregnant with mischief,
brings forth failure.
¹⁶He has opened a hole, he has dug it deep,
but he falls into the pit which he has made.
¹⁷His mischief shall recoil upon his own head;
upon the crown of his head his violence shall rebound.
¹⁸I will give thanks to the Lord for his justice,
and sing praise to the name of the Lord Most High.

PSALM 8

The Majesty of God and the Dignity of Man

¹For the leader; "upon the *gittith.*" A psalm of David.

I
²O Lord, our Lord,
how glorious is your name over all the earth!
You have exalted your majesty above the heavens.
³Out of the mouths of babes and sucklings

the enemies down (vv. 7-14). The rout of the enemies by the Lord is at the same time the judicial verdict: the psalmist is declared innocent, and the enemies are declared guilty. The punishment of the wicked comes about by the inherent force of the wicked actions themselves (vv. 15-17). The psalmist dares to put his whole life in God's hands and to rely on God alone for protection against evil and violence.

Psalm 8

The psalm is a hymn (C) in praise of God for having given human beings responsibility and dignity. One should compare Gen 1:1–2:3 and Psalm 104. Verses 4-5 declare that heaven and earth, now arranged in beauty and order, invite praise. The hymnist expresses wonder at the marvelous world crowned

you have fashioned praise because of
 your foes,
 to silence the hostile and the vengeful.
⁴When I behold your heavens, the work
 of your fingers,
 the moon and the stars which you set
 in place—
⁵What is man that you should be mind-
 ful of him,
 or the son of man that you should
 care for him?

II

⁶You have made him little less than the
 angels,
 and crowned him with glory and
 honor.
⁷You have given him rule over the
 works of your hands,
 putting all things under his feet:
⁸All sheep and oxen,
 yes, and the beasts of the field,
⁹The birds of the air, the fishes of the
 sea,
 and whatever swims the paths of the
 seas.
¹⁰O Lord, our Lord,
 how glorious is your name over all
 the earth!

PSALM 9

Thanksgiving for the Overthrow
of Hostile Nations

¹For the leader; according to *Muth labben.* A psalm
of David.

I

²I will give thanks to you, O Lord, with
 all my heart;
 I will declare all your wondrous
 deeds.

³I will be glad and exult in you;
 I will sing praise to your name, Most
 High,
⁴Because my enemies are turned back,
 overthrown and destroyed before
 you.

II

⁵For you upheld my right and my cause,
 seated on your throne, judging justly.
⁶You rebuked the nations and destroyed
 the wicked;
 their name you blotted out forever
 and ever.
⁷The enemies are ruined completely forever;
 the remembrance of the cities you up-
 rooted has perished.

III

⁸But the Lord sits enthroned forever;
 he has set up his throne for judgment.
⁹He judges the world with justice;
 he governs the peoples with equity.
¹⁰The Lord is a stronghold for the oppressed,
 a stronghold in times of distress.
¹¹They trust in you who cherish your
 name,
 for you forsake not those who seek
 you, O Lord.

IV

¹²Sing praise to the Lord enthroned in
 Zion;
 proclaim among the nations his
 deeds;
¹³For the avenger of blood has remembered;
 he has not forgotten the cry of the
 afflicted.

by human beings (vv. 6-7). Human beings stand between heaven and earth;
the world is made for them.

Psalms 9-10

The two psalms are actually one acrostic poem, that is, each section begins
with a successive letter of the twenty-two letter Hebrew alphabet. Like many
other acrostic poems, this one appears to be a series of brief, disparate state-

V

¹⁴Have pity on me, O LORD; see how I am
    afflicted by my foes,
        you who have raised me up from the
        gates of death,
¹⁵That I may declare all your praises
    and, in the gates of the daughter of
    Zion, rejoice in your salvation.

VI

¹⁶The nations are sunk in the pit they have
    made;
        in the snare they set, their foot is
        caught;
¹⁷In passing sentence, the LORD is mani-
    fest;
        the wicked are trapped by the work
        of their own hands.

VII

¹⁸To the nether world the wicked shall
    turn back,
        all the nations that forget God.
¹⁹For the needy shall not always be for-
    gotten,
        nor shall the hope of the afflicted
        forever perish.
²⁰Rise, O LORD, let not man prevail;
    let the nations be judged in your
    presence.
²¹Strike them with terror, O LORD;
    let the nations know that they are but
    men.

PSALM 10

Prayer for Help against Oppressors

I

¹Why, O LORD, do you stand aloof?
    Why hide in times of distress?
²Proudly the wicked harass the afflicted,
    who are caught in the devices the
    wicked have contrived.

II

³For the wicked man glories in his
    greed,
        and the covetous blasphemes, sets the
        LORD at nought.
⁴The wicked man boasts, "He will not
    avenge it";
        "There is no God," sums up his
        thoughts.
⁵His ways are secure at all times;
    your judgments are far from his
    mind;
    all his foes he scorns.
⁶He says in his heart, "I shall not be
    disturbed;
        from age to age I shall be without
        misfortune."
⁷His mouth is full of cursing, guile and
    deceit;
        under his tongue are mischief and
        iniquity.
⁸He lurks in ambush near the villages;
    in hiding he murders the innocent;
    his eyes spy upon the unfortunate.
⁹He waits in secret like a lion in his lair;
    he lies in wait to catch the afflicted;
    he catches the afflicted and drags
    them off in his net.
¹⁰He stoops and lies prone
    till by his violence fall the
    unfortunate.
¹¹He says in his heart, "God has forgot-
    ten;
        he hides his face, he never sees."

III

¹²Rise, O LORD! O God, lift up your
    hand!
        Forget not the afflicted!
¹³Why should the wicked man despise
    God,

ments given unity by the outer frame of the alphabet. The poem deals with
three themes: (1) the rescue of the helpless and poor from their enemies; (2)
the Lord's worldwide judgment and rule over the nations; (3) the prosperity
of the wicked, which tempts the believer. A clue to the genre may be 9:14-15,
where the psalmist offers thanksgiving (B) for being rescued by God. The

saying in his heart, "He will not
avenge it"?
[14]You do see, for you behold misery and
sorrow,
taking them in your hands.
On you the unfortunate man depends;
of the fatherless you are the helper.
[15]Break the strength of the wicked and of
the evildoer;
punish their wickedness; let them not
survive.

IV
[16]The LORD is king forever and ever;
the nations have perished out of his
land.
[17]The desire of the afflicted you hear,
O LORD;
strengthening their hearts, you pay
heed
[18]To the defense of the fatherless and the
oppressed,
that man, who is of earth, may terrify
no more.

PSALM 11

Unshaken Confidence in God

[1]For the leader. Of David.

I
In the LORD I take refuge; how can you
say to me,

"Flee to the mountain like a bird!
[2]For, see, the wicked bend the bow;
they place the arrow on the string
to shoot in the dark at the upright of
heart.
[3]When the pillars are overthrown,
what can the just man do?"

II
[4]The LORD is in his holy temple;
the LORD's throne is in heaven.
His eyes behold,
his searching glance is on mankind.
[5]The LORD searches the just and the
wicked;
the lover of violence he hates.
[6]He rains upon the wicked fiery coals and
brimstone;
a burning blast is their allotted cup.
[7]For the LORD is just, he loves just deeds;
the upright shall see his face.

PSALM 12

Prayer against Evil Tongues

[1]For the leader; "upon the eighth." A psalm of
David.

I
[2]Help, O LORD! for no one now is dutiful;
faithfulness has vanished from among
men.

psalmist, from the experience of personal salvation, points to other instances
of divine power.

Psalm 11

Some themes of lament have been made the basis of a song of trust: instead of calling out for rescue from a specific danger, one rests contentedly
in the Lord's presence. The psalmist is in danger; friends counsel flight to
the hill country, the traditional hideout for people in danger (vv. 1-2). The
chaos that, in the Bible, always lurks on the edge of God's creation is closing
in on the psalmist; his own innocence appears to offer no help (v. 3). The
psalmist chooses not to follow the advice and leave town but to seek the
Lord in the temple. He entrusts his plight to the Lord, all-powerful and all-
knowing (vv. 4-5). The psalmist's desire for the punishment of the wicked
is a desire that God's justice in its totality be done (vv. 6-7).

³Everyone speaks falsehood to his neighbor;

with smooth lips they speak, and double heart.

II

⁴May the LORD destroy all smooth lips, every boastful tongue,

⁵Those who say, "We are heroes with our tongues;

our lips are our own; who is lord over us?"

III

⁶"Because they rob the afflicted, and the needy sigh,

now will I arise," says the LORD;

"I will grant safety to him who longs for it."

IV

⁷The promises of the LORD are sure, like tried silver, freed from dross, sevenfold refined.

⁸You, O LORD, will keep us

and preserve us always from this generation,

⁹While about us the wicked strut

and in high place are the basest of men.

PSALM 13
Prayer of One in Sorrow

¹For the leader. A psalm of David.

I

²How long, O LORD? Will you utterly forget me?

How long will you hide your face from me?

³How long shall I harbor sorrow in my soul,

grief in my heart day after day?

How long will my enemy triumph over me?

⁴ Look, answer me, O LORD, my God!

II

Give light to my eyes that I may not sleep in death

⁵ lest my enemy say, "I have overcome him";

Lest my foes rejoice at my downfall

⁶ though I trusted in your kindness.

Let my heart rejoice in your salvation;

let me sing of the LORD, "He has been good to me."

Psalm 12

In this lament (A) the psalmist is caught in a human jungle, where violent people and liars oppress the just (vv. 2-3). The psalmist prays that the unjust be punished (vv. 4-5), not from a desire for revenge but from a desire to see God's will appear on earth. Verse 6 preserves the words of assurance delivered to the lamenter; usually it is not transmitted with the psalm. Verses 7-9 are statements praising the word of assurance the psalmist is willing to live by.

Psalm 13

In this lament (A) the psalmist prays to be healed lest his death be interpreted by his enemies as divine condemnation. Untimely death and serious sickness could be interpreted as the consequences of sinful conduct. The psalmist is afraid that his enemies will be vindicated. His healing would be a divine verdict in his favor.

PSALM 14

A Lament over Widespread Corruption

¹For the leader. Of David.

I

The fool says in his heart,
"There is no God."
Such are corrupt; they do abominable
deeds;
there is not one who does good.
²The LORD looks down from heaven
upon the children of men,
to see if there be one who is wise
and seeks God.
³All alike have gone astray; they have
become perverse;
there is not one who does good, not
even one.

II

⁴Will all these evildoers never learn,
they who eat up my people just as
they eat bread?
They have not called upon the LORD;
⁵ then they shall be in great fear,
for God is with the just generation.

⁶You would confound the plans of the
afflicted,
but the LORD is his refuge.

III

⁷Oh, that out of Zion would come the
salvation of Israel!
When the LORD restores the well-
being of his people,
then shall Jacob exult and Israel be
glad.

PSALM 15

The Guest of God

¹A psalm of David.

I

O LORD, who shall sojourn in your tent?
Who shall dwell on your holy mountain?

II

²He who walks blamelessly and does
justice;
who thinks the truth in his heart
³ and slanders not with his tongue;
Who harms not his fellow man,

Psalm 14

In this lament of the individual (A), duplicated in Psalm 53, the psalmist imagines the world as consisting of two types of people: "the fool" in verses 1-3 and the "just generation" in verses 4-6 (also called "my people" and "the afflicted"). The psalmist complains that the wicked persecute the community of the just (a better translation than "just generation," v. 5), while God watches from heaven. He expresses a firm hope that God will stride forth from the temple, punish the wicked, and uphold the faithful.

Psalm 15

This psalm, like Psalm 24, reflects the ceremony admitting the Israelite to the temple court. The temple was not like a church that one could enter at any time. It was God's house and could be entered only at certain times and under the proper conditions. One had to be admitted by a priest. The visitor had to answer the question of the priest at the gate: "Who may sojourn in 'your tent'?" (a traditional designation for the temple in Jerusalem). The response in verses 2-5 is a list of twelve stipulations, which sum up the covenantal obligations. Without commitment to the covenant, without conversion, one cannot enter the presence of the Lord. The psalm shows

nor takes up a reproach against his
neighbor;
[4]By whom the reprobate is despised,
while he honors those who fear the
LORD;
Who, though it be to his loss, changes
not his pledged word;
[5] who lends not his money at usury
and accepts no bribe against the innocent.

III
He who does these things
shall never be disturbed.

PSALM 16
God the Supreme Good

[1]A *miktam* of David.

I
Keep me, O God, for in you I take
refuge;
[2] I say to the LORD, "My Lord are you.
Apart from you I have no good."
[3]How wonderfully has he made me
cherish
the holy ones who are in his land!
[4]They multiply their sorrows
who court other gods.
Blood libations to them I will not pour
out,
nor will I take their names upon my
lips.

[5]O LORD, my allotted portion and my
cup,
you it is who hold fast my lot.
[6]For me the measuring lines have fallen
on pleasant sites;
fair to me indeed is my inheritance.

II
[7]I bless the LORD who counsels me;
even in the night my heart exhorts
me.
[8]I set the LORD ever before me;
with him at my right hand I shall not
be disturbed.
[9]Therefore my heart is glad and my soul
rejoices,
my body, too, abides in confidence;
[10]Because you will not abandon my soul
to the nether world,
nor will you suffer your faithful one
to undergo corruption.
[11]You will show me the path to life,
fullness of joys in your presence,
the delights at your right hand forever.

PSALM 17
Prayer against Persecutors

[1]A prayer of David.

I
Hear, O LORD, a just suit;
attend to my outcry;

that nearness to the Lord is not a matter of external ritual alone; it demands
heartfelt commitment as well.

Psalm 16

In this song of trust the psalmist takes refuge in the temple ("for in you
I take refuge," v. 1), expressing trust that the Lord, and not the so-called
gods of other nations, reigns over the land of Israel. Verses 3-6, despite corruption in verses 3-4, apparently express the psalmist's refusal to honor the
local "gods." Only the Lord, who has displaced the Canaanites and their gods
by giving the land to Israel, will receive the psalmist's worship (vv. 5-6).
Verses 7-11 express how committed the psalmist is to Israel's God, how willing to trust the Lord who has brought the people here.

hearken to my prayer from lips without deceit.

²From you let my judgment come;
    your eyes behold what is right.
³Though you test my heart, searching it
    in the night,
    though you try me with fire, you shall
    find no malice in me.
My mouth has not transgressed ⁴after
    the manner of man;
    according to the words of your lips
    I have kept the ways of the law.
⁵My steps have been steadfast in your
    paths,
    my feet have not faltered.

II

⁶I call upon you, for you will answer me,
    O God;
    incline your ear to me; hear my
    word.
⁷Show your wondrous kindness,
    O savior of those who flee
    from their foes to refuge at your
    right hand.
⁸Keep me as the apple of your eye;
    hide me in the shadow of your
    wings
⁹   from the wicked who use violence
    against me.

III

My ravenous enemies beset me;

¹⁰   they shut up their cruel hearts,
    their mouths speak proudly.
¹¹Their steps even now surround me;
    crouching to the ground, they fix their
    gaze,
¹²Like lions hungry for prey,
    like young lions lurking in hiding.

IV

¹³Rise, O LORD, confront them and cast
    them down;
    rescue me by your sword from the
    wicked,
¹⁴   by your hand, O LORD, from mortal
    men:
From mortal men whose portion in life
    is in this world,
    where with your treasures you fill
    their bellies.
Their sons are enriched
    and bequeath their abundance to
    their little ones.
¹⁵But I in justice shall behold your face;
    on waking, I shall be content in your
    presence.

PSALM 18

Thanksgiving for Help and Victory

¹For the leader. Of David, the servant of the LORD,
who sang to the LORD the words of this song when
the LORD had rescued him from the grasp of all his
enemies and from the hand of Saul.

Psalm 17

This psalm is a lament (A) of one unjustly accused who has taken refuge in the temple to await divine settlement of the case. Verses 1-2 are a prayer for vindication; verses 3-5 are an affirmation of innocence. Verses 6-9 are another prayer, more anxious than the first because of the pressure of the foe in verses 10-12. Verses 13-14 plead that the wicked be broken, and verse 15 is a serene statement of praise. The psalmist seeks a public judgment. He prays for the public punishment of his enemies so that everyone will know that he has been found innocent by the court of last resort, the Lord.

Psalm 18

Psalm 18, duplicated in 2 Sam 22, is a royal thanksgiving (B) for a military victory. The king, in the throes of his suffering, prays in the temple

A

I

²I love you, O Lord, my strength,
³ O Lord, my rock, my fortress, my
   deliverer.
My God, my rock of refuge,
   my shield, the horn of my salvation,
   my stronghold!
⁴Praised be the Lord, I exclaim,
   and I am safe from my enemies.

II

⁵The breakers of death surged round
   about me,
   the destroying floods overwhelmed
   me;
⁶The cords of the nether world en-
   meshed me,
   the snares of death overtook me.
⁷In my distress I called upon the Lord
   and cried out to my God;
From his temple he heard my voice,
   and my cry to him reached his ears.

III

⁸The earth swayed and quaked;
   the foundations of the mountains
   trembled
   and shook when his wrath flared up.
⁹Smoke rose from his nostrils,
   and a devouring fire from his mouth
   that kindled coals into flame.
¹⁰And he inclined the heavens and came
   down,
   with dark clouds under his feet.
¹¹He mounted a cherub and flew,
   borne on the wings of the wind.
¹²And he made darkness the cloak about
   him;

dark, misty rain-clouds his wrap.
¹³From the brightness of his presence
   coals were kindled to flame.
¹⁴And the Lord thundered from heaven,
   the Most High gave forth his voice;
¹⁵He sent forth his arrows to put them to
   flight,
   with frequent lightnings he routed
   them.
¹⁶Then the bed of the sea appeared,
   and the foundations of the world
   were laid bare,
At the rebuke of the Lord,
   at the blast of the wind of his wrath.
¹⁷He reached out from on high and
   grasped me;
   he drew me out of the deep waters.
¹⁸He rescued me from my mighty enemy
   and from my foes, who were too
   powerful for me.
¹⁹They attacked me in the day of my
   calamity,
   but the Lord came to my support.
²⁰He set me free in the open,
   and rescued me, because he loves me.

IV

²¹The Lord rewarded me according to my
   justice;
   according to the cleanness of my
   hands he requited me;
²²For I kept the ways of the Lord
   and was not disloyal to my God;
²³For his ordinances were all present to
   me,
   and his statutes I put not from me,
²⁴But I was wholehearted toward him,
   and I was on my guard against guilt.

(vv. 5-7), trusting not in his privileges as king but in his loyalty to God (vv. 21-25) and in his membership in God's people (v. 28).

Thanksgivings are in essence reports of divine rescue. The rescue and establishment of the king are told twice, once in mythic language (vv. 5-20) like that used in the narratives of Pss 77:14-21 and 89:10-28, and then in historical language (vv. 36-46). The outline is as follows: (I) hymnic introduction, vv. 2-4; report, vv. 5-20; conclusions regarding why the Lord effected the rescue, vv. 21-25; (II) hymnic introduction (in the second person), vv.

²⁵And the LORD requited me according to my justice,

according to the cleanness of my hands in his sight.

²⁶Toward the faithful you are faithful, toward the wholehearted you are wholehearted,

²⁷Toward the sincere you are sincere, but toward the crooked you are astute;

²⁸For lowly people you save but haughty eyes you bring low;

²⁹You indeed, O LORD, give light to my lamp;

O my God, you brighten the darkness about me;

³⁰For with your aid I run against an armed band,

and by the help of my God I leap over a wall.

³¹God's way is unerring,

the promise of the LORD is fire-tried;

he is a shield to all who take refuge in him.

B

I

³²For who is God except the LORD? Who is a rock, save our God?

³³The God who girded me with strength and kept my way unerring;

³⁴Who made my feet swift as those of hinds

and set me on the heights;

³⁵Who trained my hands for war

and my arms to bend a bow of brass.

II

³⁶You have given me your saving shield;

your right hand has upheld me,

and you have stooped to make me great.

³⁷You made room for my steps;

unwavering was my stride.

³⁸I pursued my enemies and overtook them,

nor did I turn again till I made an end of them.

³⁹I smote them and they could not rise;

they fell beneath my feet.

III

⁴⁰And you girded me with strength for war;

you subdued my adversaries beneath me.

⁴¹My enemies you put to flight before me,

and those who hated me you destroyed.

⁴²They cried for help—but no one saved them;

to the LORD—but he answered them not.

⁴³I ground them fine as the dust before the wind;

like the mud in the streets I trampled them down.

IV

⁴⁴You rescued me from the strife of the people;

you made me head over nations;

A people I had not known became my slaves;

⁴⁵ as soon as they heard me they obeyed.

The foreigners fawned and cringed before me;

⁴⁶ they staggered forth from their fortresses.

C

⁴⁷The LORD live! And blessed be my Rock!

26-35; report, vv. 36-46; proclamation of the Lord's glory to the nations, vv. 47-51.

The king represents Israel, especially to the nations (vv. 44-46, 48, 50); his victory shows to the nations the power of his patron God, Yahweh. The movement of the king from humiliation and suffering (vv. 5-7, 19) to exalta-

Extolled be God my savior.
⁴⁸O God, who granted me vengeance,
who made peoples subject to me
⁴⁹ and preserved me from my enemies,
Truly above my adversaries you exalt
me
and from the violent man you have
rescued me.
⁵⁰Therefore will I proclaim you, O LORD,
among the nations,
and I will sing praise to your name,
⁵¹You who gave great victories to your
king
and showed kindness to your
anointed,
to David and his posterity forever.

PSALM 19

God's Glory in the Heavens and in the Law

¹For the leader. A psalm of David.

A

I

²The heavens declare the glory of God,
and the firmament proclaims his
handiwork.
³Day pours out the word to day,
and night to night imparts knowl-
edge;

⁴Not a word nor a discourse
whose voice is not heard;
⁵Through all the earth their voice resounds,
and to the ends of the world, their
message.

II

He has pitched a tent there for the sun,
⁶ which comes forth like the groom
from his bridal chamber
and, like a giant, joyfully runs its
course.
⁷At one end of the heavens it comes
forth,
and its course is to their other end;
nothing escapes its heat.

B

I

⁸The law of the LORD is perfect,
refreshing the soul;
The decree of the LORD is trustworthy,
giving wisdom to the simple.
⁹The precepts of the LORD are right,
rejoicing the heart;
The command of the LORD is clear,
enlightening the eye;
¹⁰The fear of the LORD is pure,
enduring forever;
The ordinances of the LORD are true,
all of them just;

tion over the nations (vv. 44-46) makes him a living witness to the Lord's fidelity to the promises made to David and to the Lord's power.

Psalm 19

This unusual poem is a prayer that the law of the Lord, which contains such power to enlighten and enrich the person (vv. 8-11), not be denied to "your servant," the psalmist (vv. 12-15). The serene functioning of the universe expresses the wide scope and precision of the Lord's victory over what once was unbounded sea and primordial darkness, a chaos that had made human society impossible. The picture is the same as that in Psalm 104 and Gen 1.

The "glory of God" that the heavens declare in verse 1 is the power and wisdom that the Lord displays on earth in arranging them. In comparable religious literatures the sun is a judge and lawgiver; hence verses 5b-7 form

¹¹They are more precious than gold,
  than a heap of purest gold;
Sweeter also than syrup
  or honey from the comb.

II

¹²Though your servant is careful of them,
  very diligent in keeping them,
¹³Yet who can detect failings?
  Cleanse me from my unknown
  faults!
¹⁴From wanton sin especially, restrain
  your servant;
  let it not rule over me.
Then shall I be blameless and innocent
  of serious sin.
¹⁵Let the words of my mouth and the
  thought of my heart
  find favor before you,
O Lord, my rock and my redeemer.

PSALM 20

Prayer for the King in Time of War

¹For the leader. A psalm of David.

I

²The Lord answer you in time of distress;
  the name of the God of Jacob defend you!

³May he send you help from the sanctuary,
  from Zion may he sustain you.
⁴May he remember all your offerings
  and graciously accept your holocaust.
⁵May he grant you what is in your heart
  and fulfill your every plan.
⁶May we shout for joy at your victory
  and raise the standards in the name of
  our God.
The Lord grant all your requests!

II

⁷Now I know that the Lord has given
  victory to his anointed,
  that he has answered him from his
  holy heaven
  with the strength of his victorious
  right hand.
⁸Some are strong in chariots; some, in
  horses;
  but we are strong in the name of the
  Lord, our God.
⁹Though they bow down and fall,
  yet we stand erect and firm.
¹⁰O Lord, grant victory to the king,
  and answer us when we call upon
  you.

a transition to the description of the law. The law is the will of the powerful Lord visible to the servants of that Lord; hence the prayer for openness to it (vv. 12-14).

Psalm 20

The psalm is a prayer for the king, who is the representative of the people, before he and his army set out for battle. In the first section (vv. 2-6) the people ask for divine help, and in verses 7-10 they express confidence that such help will be given. A solemn promise of God's help must have been given between the two sections in the liturgy, something like the promise of Pss 12:6 and 21:9-13. The "name" as a surrogate for the Lord occurs frequently in this psalm (vv. 2b, 6b, 8b) and indeed elsewhere in the Psalter (for example, Pss 44:6; 54:8; 118:10-12; 124:8). The idea is that Yahweh dwells in heaven and the name makes Yahweh present on earth. The name is not a magic force but aids those who trust in it alone (vv. 8-9).

PSALM 21

Thanksgiving and Prayers for the King

[1]For the leader. A psalm of David.

I

[2]O LORD, in your strength the king is glad;
in your victory how greatly he rejoices!
[3]You have granted him his heart's desire;
you refused not the wish of his lips.
[4]For you welcomed him with goodly blessings,
you placed on his head a crown of pure gold.
[5]He asked life of you: you gave him length of days forever and ever.
[6]Great is his glory in your victory;
majesty and splendor you conferred upon him.
[7]For you made him a blessing forever;
you gladdened him with the joy of your presence.
[8]For the king trusts in the LORD,
and through the kindness of the Most High he stands unshaken.

II

[9]May your hand reach all your enemies,
may your right hand reach your foes!
[10]Make them burn as though in a fiery furnace,
when you appear.
May the LORD consume them in his anger;
let fire devour them.
[11]Destroy their fruit from the earth
and their posterity from among men.
[12]Though they intend evil against you,
devising plots, they cannot succeed,
[13]For you shall put them to flight;
you shall aim your shafts against them.
[14]Be extolled, O LORD, in your strength!
We will sing, chant the praise of your might.

PSALM 22

Passion and Triumph of the Messiah

[1]For the leader; according to "The hind of the dawn." A psalm of David.

A

I

[2]My God, my God, why have you forsaken me,
far from my prayer, from the words of my cry?

Psalm 21

The first part of this prayer for the king is a thanksgiving for benefits given (vv. 2-8), and the second is a promise that the king will triumph over enemies (vv. 9-14). Verse 14 is a brief prayer. The psalm may reflect a temple ceremony that celebrated the Lord's choice of the Davidic king. The king's trust in the Lord (v. 8) and his confident prayer (vv. 3, 5) enable him to receive divine gifts. Vitality and peace are not the only divine gifts visible in the king; through his military prowess the land is kept secure. Hence verses 9-14 portray the warrior-king as helped by the Lord. The heightened language is typical of the Oriental court. When kings ceased in Israel after the sixth century B.C.E., the language came to be used of a future son of David.

Psalm 22

The exceptionally powerful lament (A) freely recasts the lament structure. The complaint is duplicated. The first complaint, verses 2-12, contains

³O my God, I cry out by day, and you answer not;
   by night, and there is no relief for me.

⁴Yet you are enthroned in the holy place, O glory of Israel!

⁵In you our fathers trusted;
   they trusted, and you delivered them.

⁶To you they cried, and they escaped;
   in you they trusted, and they were not put to shame.

⁷But I am a worm, not a man;
   the scorn of men, despised by the people.

⁸All who see me scoff at me;
   they mock me with parted lips, they wag their heads:

⁹"He relied on the LORD; let him deliver him,
   let him rescue him, if he loves him."

¹⁰You have been my guide since I was first formed,
   my security at my mother's breast.

¹¹To you I was committed at birth,
   from my mother's womb you are my God.

¹²Be not far from me, for I am in distress;
   be near, for I have no one to help me.   *(II)*

¹³Many bullocks surround me;
   the strong bulls of Bashan encircle me.

¹⁴They open their mouths against me
   like ravening and roaring lions.

¹⁵I am like water poured out;
   all my bones are racked.
 My heart has become like wax
   melting away within my bosom.

¹⁶My throat is dried up like baked clay,
   my tongue cleaves to my jaws;
   to the dust of death you have brought me down.

¹⁷Indeed, many dogs surround me,
   a pack of evildoers closes in upon me;
 They have pierced my hands and my feet;

¹⁸ I can count all my bones.
 They look on and gloat over me;

¹⁹ they divide my garments among them,
   and for my vesture they cast lots.

III

²⁰But you, O LORD, be not far from me;
   O my help, hasten to aid me.

²¹Rescue my soul from the sword,
   my loneliness from the grip of the dog.

²²Save me from the lion's mouth;
   from the horns of the wild bulls, my wretched life.

B

I

²³I will proclaim your name to my brethren;
   in the midst of the assembly I will praise you:

²⁴"You who fear the LORD, praise him;
   all you descendants of Jacob, give glory to him;
   revere him, all you descendants of Israel!

²⁵For he has not spurned nor disdained the wretched man in his misery,
 Nor did he turn his face away from him, but when he cried out to him, he heard him."

²⁶So by your gift will I utter praise in the vast assembly;

two expressions of trust, verses 4-6 and 10-11, with the petition of verse 12 as the climax. The second complaint, verses 13-22, extended by vivid images, climaxes in the petition of verses 20-22. The psalm is unusual in the length of the statement of praise (vv. 23-32), which usually consists of only a verse or two at the end of the lament. The psalmist appears to have had an intense experience of God who saves, and boldly praises God "in the midst

I will fulfill my vows before those
   who fear him.
²⁷The lowly shall eat their fill;
   they who seek the LORD shall praise
     him:
   "May your hearts be ever merry!"

II

²⁸All the ends of the earth
   shall remember and turn to the LORD;
All the families of the nations
   shall bow down before him.
²⁹For dominion is the LORD's,
   and he rules the nations.
³⁰To him alone shall bow down
   all who sleep in the earth;
Before him shall bend
   all who go down into the dust. *(III)*
And to him my soul shall live;
³¹ my descendants shall serve him.
Let the coming generation be told of the
   LORD
³² that they may proclaim to a people
     yet to be born
   the justice he has shown.

PSALM 23
The Lord, Shepherd and Host

¹A psalm of David.

I

The LORD is my shepherd; I shall not
   want.
² In verdant pastures he gives me re-
     pose;
Beside restful waters he leads me;
³ he refreshes my soul.
He guides me in right paths
   for his name's sake.
⁴Even though I walk in the dark valley
   I fear no evil; for you are at my side
With your rod and your staff
   that give me courage.

II

⁵You spread the table before me
   in the sight of my foes;
You anoint my head with oil;
   my cup overflows.
⁶Only goodness and kindness follow me
   all the days of my life;

---

of the assembly" (v. 23) for coming to the poor person who hoped for salvation. The psalmist has come to know the Lord in a new way through the divine act and cannot restrain his appreciation and love.

Psalm 23

This, the most beloved psalm in the Psalter, is a song of trust. The Lord is portrayed as a shepherd, a common designation for the god or king in ancient Near Eastern poetry. The title connotes care for the people and, in the case of Israel, leadership in the Exodus-Conquest (compare Pss 78:52-55; 80; Isa 40:11 and Jer 31:10). The psalmist is so confident of the divine shepherd's leadership as to trust even when the path leads through dangerous mountain passes (v. 4a); the shepherd is there (v. 4b). The Exodus-Conquest ended with Israel safe in the Lord's land. That journey is concluded in the psalm with a banquet. The enemies that tried to hinder the journey toward the divine dwelling are shamed as they see God's favor bestowed on the psalmist in the temple.

Psalm 24

Like Psalm 15, this psalm appears to have accompanied the ceremony of admittance to the temple on a solemn occasion (compare v. 3 with Ps 15:1,

And I shall dwell in the house of the
 Lord
 for years to come.

PSALM 24

The Lord's Solemn Entry into Zion

[1]A psalm of David.

I

The Lord's are the earth and its fullness;
 the world and those who dwell in it.
[2]For he founded it upon the seas
 and established it upon the rivers.

II

[3]Who can ascend the mountain of the
 Lord?
 or who may stand in his holy place?
[4]He whose hands are sinless, whose
 heart is clean,
 who desires not what is vain,
 nor swears deceitfully to his neighbor.
[5]He shall receive a blessing from the
 Lord,
 a reward from God his savior.
[6]Such is the race that seeks for him,
 that seeks the face of the God of
 Jacob.

III

[7]Lift up, O gates, your lintels;
 reach up, you ancient portals,

that this king of glory may come in!
[8]Who is this king of glory?
 The Lord, strong and mighty,
 the Lord, mighty in battle.
[9]Lift up, O gates, your lintels;
 reach up, you ancient portals,
 that the king of glory may come in!
[10]Who is this king of glory?
 The Lord of hosts; he is the king of
 glory.

PSALM 25

Prayer for Guidance and Help

[1]Of David.

I

To you I lift up my soul,
 O Lord, [2]my God.
In you I trust; let me not be put to
 shame,
 let not my enemies exult over me.
[3]No one who waits for you shall be put
 to shame;
 those shall be put to shame who
 heedlessly break faith.
[4]Your ways, O Lord, make known to
 me;
 teach me your paths,
[5]Guide me in your truth and teach me,
 for you are God my savior,
 and for you I wait all the day.

and vv. 4-6 with Ps 15:2-5). One had to affirm commitment to the covenant
in order to appear before the Lord. Verses 1-2 and 7-10 reflect the ceremony.
In the first verses the Lord's sovereignty over the created world is celebrated.
People of that time imagined that the earth was suspended over vast waters,
supported by great pillars. Verses 7-10 describe the procession of the Lord
approaching the temple in triumph. Two choirs, singing antiphonally, iden-
tify the approaching Lord (perhaps represented by the ark carried by priests).
The psalm invites worshipers to commit themselves anew to their Creator-
Lord as they join in the triumphant procession.

Psalm 25

The psalm is an acrostic poem, each verse beginning with a successive
letter of the Hebrew alphabet. Acrostic psalms are often a series of uncon-
nected statements; poetic unity is supplied by the extrinsic device of the suc-

[6]Remember that your compassion, O
    Lord,
  and your kindness are from of old.
[7]The sins of my youth and my frailties
    remember not;
  in your kindness remember me,
  because of your goodness, O Lord.

II
[8]Good and upright is the Lord;
  thus he shows sinners the way.
[9]He guides the humble to justice,
  he teaches the humble his way.
[10]All the paths of the Lord are kindness
    and constancy
  toward those who keep his covenant
    and his decrees.
[11]For your name's sake, O Lord,
  you will pardon my guilt, great as it
    is.
[12]When a man fears the Lord,
  he shows him the way he should
    choose.
[13]He abides in prosperity,
  and his descendants inherit the land.
[14]The friendship of the Lord is with those
    who fear him,
  and his covenant, for their instruc-
    tion.
[15]My eyes are ever toward the Lord,
  for he will free my feet from the
    snare.

III
[16]Look toward me, and have pity on me,
  for I am alone and afflicted.
[17]Relieve the troubles of my heart,
  and bring me out of my distress.
[18]Put an end to my affliction and my
    suffering,
  and take away all my sins.
[19]Behold, my enemies are many,
  and they hate me violently.
[20]Preserve my life, and rescue me;
  let me not be put to shame, for I take
    refuge in you.
[21]Let integrity and uprightness preserve
    me,
  because I wait for you, O Lord.
[22]Redeem Israel, O God,
  from all its distress!

PSALM 26
Prayer of an Innocent Man

[1]Of David.

I
Do me justice, O Lord! for I have
    walked in integrity,
  and in the Lord I trust without
    wavering.
[2]Search me, O Lord, and try me;
  test my soul and my heart.

cessive letters. Despite the looseness, the psalm is a lament (A) containing complaints mixed with pleas to be delivered from enemies (vv. 1-2, 16-22). The psalmist is acutely conscious of having sinned; there is no claim of innocence as in some other psalms. The psalmist's fragility leads to reiterated prayer to be led along the path taken by the friends of God, where one is safe from one's enemies.

Psalm 26

Psalm 26 is often classified as a lament, but the enemies here do not attack, as in laments. Probably the song was sung by the priests who ritually washed before they offered sacrifice. Exod 30:20-21 states: ". . . when they approach the altar in their ministry, to offer an oblation to the Lord, they must wash their hands and feet, lest they die." The psalm was suitable for use by all who sought God's protection as they entered the temple. Verses

II

³For your kindness is before my eyes,
and I walk in your truth.
⁴I stay not with worthless men,
nor do I consort with hypocrites.
⁵I hate the assembly of evildoers,
and with the wicked I will not stay.
⁶I wash my hands in innocence,
and I go around your altar, O Lord,
⁷Giving voice to my thanks,
and recounting all your wondrous
deeds.
⁸O Lord, I love the house in which you
dwell,
the tenting-place of your glory.

III

⁹Gather not my soul with those of
sinners,
nor with men of blood my life.
¹⁰On their hands are crimes,
and their right hands are full of
bribes.
¹¹But I walk in integrity;
redeem me, and have pity on me.
¹²My foot stands on level ground;
in the assemblies I will bless the Lord.

PSALM 27
Trust in God

¹Of David.

A

I

The Lord is my light and my salvation;
whom should I fear?
The Lord is my life's refuge;
of whom should I be afraid?
²When evildoers come at me
to devour my flesh,
My foes and my enemies
themselves stumble and fall.
³Though an army encamp against me,
my heart will not fear;
Though war be waged upon me,
even then will I trust.

II

⁴One thing I ask of the Lord;
this I seek:
To dwell in the house of the Lord
all the days of my life,
That I may gaze on the loveliness of the
Lord
and contemplate his temple.

1-3, echoed in verses 11-12, remind God of past sincerity while asking for further purification. Verses 4-5, matched in verses 9-10, make a sharp distinction between the wicked and the just; the psalmist prays to be of the company of the righteous. Verses 6-8 are the central panel and the center of the poem. The psalmist expresses the inner meaning of the ritual: joy before the transcendent God who draws near.

Psalm 27

Tradition has handed down the two sections of the psalm, verses 1-6 and verses 7-14, as one psalm, though each part could be understood as complete in itself. The first section is a song of trust, and the second a lament (A). A common theme unites the poem: those who seek the Lord in the temple are protected (see vv. 4-6 and v. 9). Verses 1-3 remind one of another song of trust, Psalm 23, in which the psalmist's conviction of the Lord's protecting presence is intense. Verses 4-6 refer to the temple and the delight and safety to be found there in the midst of a broken and dangerous world. In the liturgy the living, victorious God appears. Verses 7-13 are an anxious prayer that the saving presence not be withheld from the psalmist, who is

⁵For he will hide me in his abode
  in the day of trouble;
He will conceal me in the shelter of his
  tent,
    he will set me high upon a rock.
⁶Even now my head is held high
  above my enemies on every side.
And I will offer in his tent
  sacrifices with shouts of gladness;
I will sing and chant praise to the Lord.

B

I

⁷Hear, O Lord, the sound of my call;
  have pity on me, and answer me.
⁸Of you my heart speaks; you my
  glance seeks;
    your presence, O Lord, I seek.
⁹Hide not your face from me;
  do not in anger repel your servant.
You are my helper: cast me not off;
  forsake me not, O God my savior.
¹⁰Though my father and mother forsake
  me,
    yet will the Lord receive me.

II

¹¹Show me, O Lord, your way, and lead
  me on a level path,
    because of my adversaries.
¹²Give me not up to the wishes of my
  foes;
    for false witnesses have risen up
    against me,
    and such as breathe out violence.

¹³I believe that I shall see the bounty of
  the Lord
    in the land of the living.
¹⁴Wait for the Lord with courage;
  be stouthearted, and wait for the
  Lord.

PSALM 28
Petition and Thanksgiving

¹Of David.

I

To you, O Lord, I call;
  O my Rock, be not deaf to me,
Lest, if you heed me not,
  I become one of those going down
  into the pit.
²Hear the sound of my pleading, when I
  cry to you,
    lifting up my hands toward your holy
    shrine.
³Drag me not away with the wicked,
  with those who do wrong,
Who speak civilly to their neighbors
  though evil is in their hearts.
⁴Repay them for their deeds,
  for the evil of their doings.
For the work of their hands repay them;
  give them their deserts.
⁵Because they consider not
  the deeds of the Lord nor the work of
  his hands,
    may he tear them down and not build
    them up.

in danger from enemies. Verse 14 is the statement of praise that customarily ends such psalms.

Psalm 28

In this lament (A) the statement of praise (vv. 6-8), uttered after the priest's words of assurance (not transmitted in this or in most psalms), is exceptionally lengthy and vigorous. The psalmist turns toward the temple, the unshakable center of an otherwise dangerous universe (v. 1-2). "Those going down into the pit" in verse 1b is a stereotyped expression for those overcome by death and descending to Sheol, the shadowy nether world. Verses 3-5 are a petition that God judge publicly. The psalmist knows that evildoers are heading toward annihilation as a result of their actions; by pray-

II

6Blessed be the LORD,
   for he has heard the sound of my
      pleading;
7   the LORD is my strength and my
      shield.
 In him my heart trusts, and I find help;
   then my heart exults, and with my
      song I give him thanks.

III

8The LORD is the strength of his people,
   the saving refuge of his anointed.
9Save your people, and bless your in-
      heritance;
   feed them, and carry them forever!

PSALM 29

God's Majesty in the Storm

1A psalm of David.

I

 Give to the LORD, you sons of God,
   give to the LORD glory and praise,
2Give to the LORD the glory due his
      name;
   adore the LORD in holy attire.

II

3The voice of the LORD is over the waters,
   the God of glory thunders,
   the LORD, over vast waters.
4The voice of the LORD is mighty;
   the voice of the LORD is majestic.
5The voice of the LORD breaks the cedars,
   the LORD breaks the cedars of Leba-
      non.
6He makes Lebanon leap like a calf
   and Sirion like a young bull.
7The voice of the LORD strikes fiery
      flames;
8   the voice of the LORD shakes the
      desert,
   the LORD shakes the wilderness of
      Kadesh.
9The voice of the LORD twists the oaks
   and strips the forests,
   and in his temple all say, "Glory!"

III

10The LORD is enthroned above the flood;
   the LORD is enthroned as king forever.
11May the LORD give strength to his
      people;
   may the LORD bless his people with
      peace!

ing for their destruction he is lining himself up with the just and is thus able to claim God's promised protection of the just. The last verses express the psalmist's acceptance of the word of assurance as effective divine words. The psalmist does not neglect to pray for the people also (v. 9).

Psalm 29

The hymn (C—see p. 7) invites the members of the heavenly court to join in giving glory to Yahweh, the sole God (vv. 1-2). The "glory and strength [rather than praise]" that they give is their recognition that Yahweh alone is king (v. 10), who alone has shaped the world by means of victory. The weapons in that victory are those of the storm-god—thunder ("the voice of the Lord," in verses 3-9), lightning, and wind. With these the Lord has vanquished the forces hostile to civilization and has made them part of the world of men and women. Verse 11 prays that the Lord will impart the power that shaped the universe to the king of Israel and, through that king, to the people. Thus the hymn celebrates the power of the Lord and the sharing of that creative power with the people of God.

PSALM 30

Thanksgiving for Deliverance from Death

¹A psalm. A song for the dedication of the temple. Of David.

²I will extol you, O LORD, for you drew me clear
  and did not let my enemies rejoice over me.

A

³O LORD, my God,
  I cried out to you and you healed me.
⁴O LORD, you brought me up from the nether world;
  you preserved me from among those going down into the pit.
⁵Sing praise to the LORD, you his faithful ones,
  and give thanks to his holy name.
⁶For his anger lasts but a moment;
  a lifetime, his good will.
At nightfall, weeping enters in,
  but with the dawn, rejoicing.

B

I

⁷Once, in my security, I said,
  "I shall never be disturbed."
⁸O LORD, in your good will you had endowed me with majesty and strength;
  but when you hid your face I was terrified.

II

⁹To you, O LORD, I cried out;
  with the LORD I pleaded:
¹⁰"What gain would there be from my lifeblood,
  from my going down into the grave?
Would dust give you thanks
  or proclaim your faithfulness?
¹¹Hear, O LORD, and have pity on me;
  O LORD, be my helper."

III

¹²You changed my mourning into dancing;
  you took off my sackcloth and clothed me with gladness,
¹³That my soul might sing praise to you without ceasing;
  O LORD, my God, forever will I give you thanks.

PSALM 31

Prayer in Distress and Thanksgiving for Escape

¹For the leader. A psalm of David.

I

²In you, O LORD, I take refuge;
  let me never be put to shame.
In your justice rescue me,

Psalm 30

In this thanksgiving (B—see p. 7) praise is given to God for rescue from near fatal illness. Verses 2-4 describe the divine mercy, the snatching of the sick person from the annihilating power of death. As often in thanksgivings, the one rescued is so relieved and delighted that he teaches and exhorts the assembly to trust the saving Lord (vv. 5-6). The assembly learns about the psalmist's inner journey, from his unthinking self-confidence (vv. 7-8a) to his panicky pleas and bargaining when illness struck (vv. 8b-11). Verses 12-13 express the delight of one who has experienced God's favor and forgiveness.

Psalm 31

The psalm is primarily a lament (A), with elements of a thanksgiving (the rescue seems to have already taken place according to verses 8-9 and 20-21)

³ incline your ear to me,
   make haste to deliver me!
 Be my rock of refuge,
   a stronghold to give me safety.
⁴You are my rock and my fortress;
   for your name's sake you will lead
   and guide me.
⁵You will free me from the snare they set
   for me,
   for you are my refuge.
⁶Into your hands I commend my spirit;
   you will redeem me, O LORD, O faithful God.
⁷You hate those who worship vain idols,
   but my trust is in the LORD.
⁸I will rejoice and be glad of your kindness,
   when you have seen my affliction
   and watched over me in my distress,
⁹Not shutting me up in the grip of the enemy
   but enabling me to move about at large.

II

¹⁰Have pity on me, O LORD, for I am in distress;
   with sorrow my eye is consumed; my soul also, and my body.
¹¹For my life is spent with grief
   and my years with sighing;
 My strength has failed through affliction,
   and my bones are consumed.
¹²For all my foes I am an object of reproach,
   a laughingstock to my neighbors, and a dread to my friends;
   they who see me abroad flee from me.

¹³I am forgotten like the unremembered dead;
   I am like a dish that is broken.
¹⁴I hear the whispers of the crowd, that frighten me from every side,
   as they consult together against me,
   plotting to take my life.
¹⁵But my trust is in you, O LORD;
   I say, "You are my God."
¹⁶In your hands is my destiny; rescue me from the clutches of my enemies and my persecutors.
¹⁷Let your face shine upon your servant; save me in your kindness.
¹⁸O LORD, let me not be put to shame, for I call upon you;
   let the wicked be put to shame; let them be reduced to silence in the nether world.
¹⁹Let dumbness strike their lying lips
   that speak insolence against the just in pride and scorn.

III

²⁰How great is the goodness, O LORD,
   which you have in store for those who fear you,
 And which, toward those who take refuge in you,
   you show in the sight of men.
²¹You hide them in the shelter of your presence
   from the plottings of men;
 You screen them within your abode
   from the strife of tongues.
²²Blessed be the LORD whose wondrous kindness
   he has shown me in a fortified city.
²³Once I said in my anguish,
   "I am cut off from your sight";

and a song of trust (vv. 4, 6, and 15-16). Moreover, the psalm seems to unfold in two narrative phrases, verses 2-9 and 10-25, probably an instance of the parallelism characteristic of Semitic poetry.

As usual in laments, the affliction is couched in general terms. The psalmist is in danger of being overwhelmed by evil people. In all these pains the psalmist turns to the "faithful God" (v. 6), whose being is described in verses 20-21.

Yet you heard the sound of my pleading
    when I cried out to you.
²⁴Love the LORD, all you his faithful
        ones!
    The LORD keeps those who are con-
        stant,
    but more than requites those who act
        proudly.
²⁵Take courage and be stouthearted,
    all you who hope in the LORD.

PSALM 32
Remission of Sin

¹Of David. A *maskil*.

I

Happy is he whose fault is taken away,
    whose sin is covered.
²Happy the man to whom the LORD
        imputes not guilt,
    in whose spirit there is no guile.

II

³As long as I would not speak, my bones
        wasted away
    with my groaning all the day,
⁴For day and night your hand was heavy
        upon me;
    my strength was dried up as by the
        heat of summer.
⁵Then I acknowledged my sin to you,
    my guilt I covered not.

I said, "I confess my faults to the LORD,"
    and you took away the guilt of my
        sin.
⁶For this shall every faithful man pray to
        you
    in time of stress.
Though deep waters overflow,
    they shall not reach him.

⁷You are my shelter; from distress you
        will preserve me;
    with glad cries of freedom you will
        ring me round.

III

⁸I will instruct you and show you the
        way you should walk;
    I will counsel you, keeping my eye
        on you.
⁹Be not senseless like horses or mules:
    with bit and bridle their temper must
        be curbed,
    else they will not come near you.

IV

¹⁰Many are the sorrows of the wicked,
    but kindness surrounds him who
        trusts in the LORD.

¹¹Be glad in the LORD and rejoice, you
        just;
    exult, all you upright of heart.

Psalm 32

This thanksgiving (B) is the second of the seven Penitential Psalms of
church tradition (see p. 11). The psalmist reports the Lord's rescue: sin
once reigned over him, body and soul. Sin here, as often in the Bible, is not
only the personal act of rebellion against God but also the consequences of
that act—the waning of vitality and frustration.

Burdened with the consequences of personal folly, the psalmist declares
everyone blessed who has been forgiven by God (vv. 1-2). Verses 3-4 describe his past refusal to open himself up to the Lord, and verses 5-7, the
happy result of letting God be the forgiving God. In verses 8-11 the psalmist
becomes a teacher, sharing with the assembly the fruits of personal experience:
the wicked (v. 10), who do not open themselves to the forgiving Lord, are
unhappy, but those who trust in the merciful God are filled with gladness.

PSALM 33
Praise of the Lord's Power and Providence

I

¹Exult, you just, in the LORD;
  praise from the upright is fitting.
²Give thanks to the LORD on the harp;
  with the ten-stringed lyre chant his
  praises.
³Sing to him a new song;
  pluck the strings skillfully, with
  shouts of gladness.
⁴For upright is the word of the LORD,
  and all his works are trustworthy.
⁵He loves justice and right;
  of the kindness of the LORD the
  earth is full.

II

⁶By the word of the LORD the heavens
  were made;
  by the breath of his mouth all their
  host.
⁷He gathers the waters of the sea as in a
  flask;
  in cellars he confines the deep.

III

⁸Let all the earth fear the LORD;
  let all who dwell in the world revere
  him.

⁹For he spoke, and it was made;
  he commanded, and it stood forth.
¹⁰The LORD brings to nought the plans of
  nations;
  he foils the designs of peoples.
¹¹But the plan of the LORD stands forever;
  the design of his heart, through all
  generations.
¹²Happy the nation whose God is the
  LORD,
  the people he has chosen for his own
  inheritance.

IV

¹³From heaven the LORD looks down;
  he sees all mankind.
¹⁴From his fixed throne he beholds
  all who dwell on the earth,
¹⁵He who fashioned the heart of each,
  he who knows all their works.

V

¹⁶A king is not saved by a mighty army,
  nor is a warrior delivered by great
  strength.
¹⁷Useless is the horse for safety;
  great though its strength, it cannot
  provide escape.
¹⁸But see, the eyes of the LORD are upon
  those who fear him,
  upon those who hope for his kindness,

Psalm 33

In this wonderfully complex hymn (C) the just are called to praise God, who made the world by a mere word (vv. 4 and 9). The world is portrayed as three-tiered: the heavenly tier and its inhabitants, the cosmic waters that surround the universe, the earthly tier and its inhabitants (vv. 6-9). The words and plans of human beings, in contrast to God's word, effect nothing (vv. 10-11).

Of all the wonders created by the word of the Lord, human beings are special because they are free to plan and to revere the Lord (vv. 8, 10-11). Verses 12-19 sketch how a people and its king are to conduct themselves on the earth God created. Their greatness consists in God's choice of them and God's clear vision into their hearts (vv. 12-15), in their leader's acknowledgment of the Lord (vv. 16-17). The psalmist directs the people to trust in the One who makes the people great (vv. 20-22).

¹⁹To deliver them from death
  and preserve them in spite of famine.

VI

²⁰Our soul waits for the Lᴏʀᴅ,
  who is our help and our shield,
²¹For in him our hearts rejoice;
  in his holy name we trust.
²²May your kindness, O Lᴏʀᴅ, be upon us
  who have put our hope in you.

PSALM 34

Praise of God, the Protector of the Just

¹Of David, when he feigned madness before Abimelech, who forced him to depart.

I

²I will bless the Lᴏʀᴅ at all times;
  his praise shall be ever in my mouth.
³Let my soul glory in the Lᴏʀᴅ;
  the lowly will hear me and be glad.
⁴Glorify the Lᴏʀᴅ with me,
  let us together extol his name.

II

⁵I sought the Lᴏʀᴅ, and he answered me
  and delivered me from all my fears.
⁶Look to him that you may be radiant
  with joy,
  and your faces may not blush with
  shame.
⁷When the afflicted man called out, the
  Lᴏʀᴅ heard,
  and from all his distress he saved him.
⁸The angel of the Lᴏʀᴅ encamps
  around those who fear him, and delivers them.

⁹Taste and see how good the Lᴏʀᴅ is;
  happy the man who takes refuge in
  him.
¹⁰Fear the Lᴏʀᴅ, you his holy ones,
  for nought is lacking to those who
  fear him.
¹¹The great grow poor and hungry;
  but those who seek the Lᴏʀᴅ want for
  no good thing.

III

¹²Come, children, hear me;
  I will teach you the fear of the Lᴏʀᴅ.
¹³Which of you desires life,
  and takes delight in prosperous days?
¹⁴Keep your tongue from evil
  and your lips from speaking guile;
¹⁵Turn from evil, and do good;
  seek peace, and follow after it.
¹⁶The Lᴏʀᴅ has eyes for the just,
  and ears for their cry.
¹⁷The Lᴏʀᴅ confronts the evildoers,
  to destroy remembrance of them from
  the earth.
¹⁸When the just cry out, the Lᴏʀᴅ hears
  them,
  and from all their distress he res-
  cues them.
¹⁹The Lᴏʀᴅ is close to the brokenhearted;
  and those who are crushed in spirit he
  saves.
²⁰Many are the troubles of the just man,
  but out of them all the Lᴏʀᴅ delivers
  him;
²¹He watches over all his bones;
  not one of them shall be broken.

Psalm 34

This thanksgiving (B) is in acrostic form, each line beginning with a successive letter of the Hebrew alphabet. In this psalm one letter is missing and two are in reverse order. The psalmist, fresh from the experience of being saved by the Lord from danger (vv. 5, 7), calls on all the "lowly" (vv. 3b-4) to praise the Lord, who saves the poor who trust. The "lowly" are the defenseless, who have only the Lord to turn to. If the defenseless person prays, the Lord will hear and that person will become powerful (vv. 7-11). In the second part of the poem, the psalmist, taught true wisdom by his suffering,

²²Vice slays the wicked,
> and the enemies of the just pay for
> their guilt.

²³But the LORD redeems the lives of his
servants;
> no one incurs guilt who takes refuge
> in him.

PSALM 35

Prayer for Help against Unjust Enemies

¹Of David.

I

Fight, O LORD, against those who fight
me;
> war against those who make war
> upon me.

²Take up the shield and buckler,
> and rise up in my defense.

³Brandish the lance, and block the way
in the face of my pursuers;
Say to my soul,
> "I am your salvation."

⁴Let those be put to shame and disgraced
> who seek my life;
Let those be turned back and confounded
> who plot evil against me.

⁵Let them be like chaff before the wind,
> with the angel of the LORD driving
> them on.

⁶Let their way be dark and slippery,
> with the angel of the LORD pursuing
> them.

II

⁷For without cause they set their snare
for me,
> without cause they dug a pit against
> my life.

⁸Let ruin come upon them unawares,
> and let the snare they have set catch
> them;
> into the pit they have dug let them
> fall.

⁹But I will rejoice in the LORD,
> I will be joyful because of his salva-
> tion.

¹⁰All my being shall say,
> "O LORD, who is like you,
The rescuer of the afflicted man from
those too strong for him,
> of the afflicted and the needy from
> their despoilers?"

¹¹Unjust witnesses have risen up;
> things I knew not of, they lay to my
> charge.

¹²They have repaid me evil for good,
> bringing bereavement to my soul.

III

¹³But I, when they were ill, put on sackcloth;
> I afflicted myself with fasting
> and poured forth prayers within my
> bosom.

¹⁴As though it were a friend of mine, or a
brother, I went about;
> like one bewailing a mother, I was
> bowed down in mourning.

now teaches the assembly (vv. 12-23). Anyone who is wise will, by right
conduct, join the company of the righteous and thus enjoy God's favor.

Psalm 35

In this lament (A) a person unjustly accused by former friends takes refuge in the court of last resort, coming before the divine judge (v. 1) and all-
seeing witness (v. 22). Verses 1-8 are a prayer for justice, asking that the
evildoers be publicly exposed as such by their punishment. Verses 9-10 are
a kind of anticipatory thanksgiving, praising God in advance of the rescue.
Verses 11-16 extend the complaint of verse 7: friends have done it! Verses

¹⁵Yet when I stumbled they were glad
and gathered together;
they gathered together striking me unawares.
They tore at me without ceasing;
¹⁶ they put me to the test; they mocked
me,
gnashing their teeth at me.

IV
¹⁷O Lord, how long will you look on?
Save me from the roaring beasts;
from the lions, my only life.
¹⁸I will give you thanks in the vast assembly,
in the mighty throng I will praise you.
¹⁹Let not my unprovoked enemies rejoice
over me;
let not my undeserved foes wink
knowingly.
²⁰For civil words they speak not,
but against the peaceful in the land
they fashion treacherous speech.
²¹And they open wide their mouths
against me,
saying, "Aha! aha! We saw him with
our own eyes!"
²²You, O Lord, have seen; be not silent;
Lord, be not far from me!
²³Awake, and be vigilant in my defense;
in my cause, my God and my Lord.
²⁴Do me justice, because you are just,
O Lord;
my God, let them not rejoice over me.

²⁵Let them not say in their hearts, "Aha!
This is what we wanted!"
Let them not say, "We have swal-
lowed him up!"
²⁶Let all be put to shame and confounded
who are glad at my misfortune.
Let those be clothed with shame and
disgrace
who glory over me.
²⁷But let those shout for joy and be glad
who favor my just cause;
And may they ever say, "The Lord be
glorified;
he wills the prosperity of his servant!"
²⁸Then my tongue shall recount your
justice,
your praise, all the day.

PSALM 36
Human Wickedness
and Divine Providence

¹For the leader. Of David, the servant of the Lord.
I
²Sin speaks to the wicked man in his
heart;
there is no dread of God before his
eyes,
³For he beguiles himself with the thought
that his guilt will not be found out or
hated.
⁴The words of his mouth are empty and
false;

17-21 press for speedy assistance, and verses 22-26, like verses 1-8, pray for the destruction of the psalmist's unjust persecutors. The modern reader, offended perhaps by the vindictive tone of the psalm, should remember that the psalmist asks for *public* redress of a *public* injustice and leaves in God's own hands the carrying out of the work of justice.

Psalm 36

This lament (A) is the prayer of one who feels threatened by "evildoers," people who attack the just (v. 13). The psalmist depicts the wicked in all their arrogance and moral obtuseness (vv. 2-5), and then comes before the just and merciful God, who punishes such evildoers and draws near in tender-

he has ceased to understand how to do good.

⁵He plans wickedness in his bed;
  he sets out on a way that is not good,
  with no repugnance for evil.

II

⁶O Lᴏʀᴅ, your kindness reaches to heaven;
  your faithfulness, to the clouds.

⁷Your justice is like the mountains of God;
  your judgments, like the mighty deep;
  man and beast you save, O Lᴏʀᴅ.

⁸How precious is your kindness, O God!
  The children of men take refuge in the shadow of your wings;

⁹They have their fill of the prime gifts of your house;
  from your delightful stream you give them to drink.

¹⁰For with you is the fountain of life,
  and in your light we see light.

III

¹¹Keep up your kindness toward your friends,
  your just defense of the upright of heart.

¹²Let not the foot of the proud overtake me
  nor the hand of the wicked disquiet me.

¹³See how the evildoers have fallen;
  they are thrust down and cannot rise.

PSALM 37

The Fate of Sinners and the Reward of the Just

¹Of David.
Be not vexed over evildoers,
  nor jealous of those who do wrong;

²For like grass they quickly wither,
  and like green herbs they wilt.

³Trust in the Lᴏʀᴅ and do good,
  that you may dwell in the land and enjoy security.

⁴Take delight in the Lᴏʀᴅ,
  and he will grant you your heart's requests.

⁵Commit to the Lᴏʀᴅ your way;
  trust in him, and he will act.

⁶He will make justice dawn for you like the light;
  bright as the noonday shall be your vindication.

⁷Leave it to the Lᴏʀᴅ,
  and wait for him;
Be not vexed at the successful path
  of the man who does malicious deeds.

⁸Give up your anger, and forsake wrath;
  be not vexed, it will only harm you.

⁹For evildoers shall be cut off,
  but those who wait for the Lᴏʀᴅ shall possess the land.

¹⁰Yet a little while, and the wicked man shall be no more;
  though you mark his place he will not be there.

ness to the beleaguered just (vv. 6-10). Verses 8-10 show the closeness of the saving Lord in the temple service. "The shadow of your wings" refers to the cherubim in the holy of holies. "They have their fill of the prime gifts of your house" reads literally, "they are sated with the fat [of the temple sacrifices]."

Psalm 37

A wise teacher speaks to disciples troubled by the prosperity of the unjust and the hiddenness of God. The psalm is an acrostic; its statements are unified by the extrinsic device of beginning the verses with successive letters of the Hebrew alphabet. In the culture of the time, lore was handed down

¹¹But the meek shall possess the land,
    they shall delight in abounding peace.
¹²The wicked man plots against the just
    and gnashes his teeth at them;
¹³But the LORD laughs at him,
    for he sees that his day is coming.
¹⁴A sword the wicked draw; they bend
    their bow
        to bring down the afflicted and the
        poor,
        to slaughter those whose path is
        right.
¹⁵But their swords shall pierce their own
    hearts,
    and their bows shall be broken.
¹⁶Better is the scanty store of the just
    than the great wealth of the wicked,
¹⁷For the power of the wicked shall be
    broken,
    but the LORD supports the just.
¹⁸The LORD watches over the lives of the
    wholehearted;
    their inheritance lasts forever.
¹⁹They are not put to shame in an evil
    time;
    in days of famine they have plenty.
²⁰But the wicked perish,
    and the enemies of the LORD, like the
    beauty of the meadows,
    vanish; like smoke they vanish.
²¹The wicked man borrows and does
    not repay;
    the just man is kindly and gives,
²²But those whom he blesses shall possess
    the land,
    while those he curses shall be cut off.
²³By the LORD are the steps of a man
    made firm,
    and he approves his way.

²⁴Though he fall, he does not lie pros-
    trate,
    for the hand of the LORD sustains
    him.
²⁵Neither in my youth, nor now that I am
    old,
    have I seen a just man forsaken
    nor his descendants begging bread.
²⁶All the day he is kindly and lends,
    and his descendants shall be blessed.
²⁷Turn from evil and do good,
    that you may abide forever;
²⁸For the LORD loves what is right,
    and forsakes not his faithful ones.
Criminals are destroyed,
    and the posterity of the wicked is cut
    off.
²⁹The just shall possess the land
    and dwell in it forever.
³⁰The mouth of the just man tells of
    wisdom
    and his tongue utters what is right.
³¹The law of his God is in his heart,
    and his steps do not falter.
³²The wicked man spies on the just,
    and seeks to slay him.
³³The LORD will not leave him in his
    power
    nor let him be condemned when he is
    on trial.
³⁴Wait for the LORD,
    and keep his way;
He will promote you to ownership of
    the land;
    when the wicked are destroyed, you
    shall look on.
³⁵I saw a wicked man, fierce,
    and stalwart as a flourishing, age-old
    tree.

orally, its authority being based upon the stature and experience of the teacher. Priests, kings, royal officials, and parents were expected to hand on what they had received.

To people troubled by the fact that the unjust victimize the just without being punished, the wise teacher asserts that the disturbing situation is only temporary; the Lord will punish the wicked in the future. In the view of the psalm, people place themselves in the ranks of the unjust by their actions

³⁶Yet as I passed by, lo! he was no more;
    I sought him, but he could not be
    found.
³⁷Watch the wholehearted man, and
    mark the upright;
    for there is a future for the man of
    peace.
³⁸Sinners shall all alike be destroyed;
    the future of the wicked shall be cut
    off.
³⁹The salvation of the just is from the
    LORD;
    he is their refuge in time of distress.
⁴⁰And the LORD helps them and delivers
    them;
    he delivers them from the wicked and
    saves them,
    because they take refuge in him.

PSALM 38

Prayer of an Afflicted Sinner

¹A psalm of David. For remembrance.

I

²O LORD, in your anger punish me not,
    in your wrath chastise me not;
³For your arrows have sunk deep in me,
    and your hand has come down upon
    me.
⁴There is no health in my flesh because of
    your indignation;
    there is no wholeness in my bones
    because of my sin,
⁵For my iniquities have overwhelmed
    me;

they are like a heavy burden, beyond
    my strength.

II

⁶Noisome and festering are my sores
    because of my folly,
⁷I am stooped and bowed down pro-
    foundly;
    all the day I go in mourning,
⁸For my loins are filled with burning
    pains;
    there is no health in my flesh.
⁹I am numbed and severely crushed;
    I roar with anguish of heart.
¹⁰O LORD, all my desire is before you;
    from you my groaning is not hid.
¹¹My heart throbs; my strength forsakes
    me;
    the very light of my eyes has failed
    me.
¹²My friends and my companions stand
    back because of my affliction;
    my neighbors stand afar off.
¹³Men lay snares for me seeking my life;
    they look to my misfortune, they
    speak of ruin,
    treachery they talk of all the day.

III

¹⁴But I am like a deaf man, hearing not,
    like a dumb man who opens not his
    mouth.
¹⁵I am become like a man who neither
    hears
    nor has in his mouth a retort.

and attitudes. Each path of life, or "way," has its own inherent dynamism—eventual frustration for the wicked, eventual reward for the just. Good things, especially symbolized by the land, lie in the future for the just, a theme with echoes in the New Testament beatitudes. Let the just wait for the Lord!

Psalm 38

In this psalm of lament (A), one of the Penitential Psalms (see p. 11), the psalmist is afflicted with deadly sickness, commonly a sign of divine disfavor. People believed that actions brought consequences of themselves: health, reputation, and prosperity came from good actions; illness, loss of face and poverty followed from evil actions. The psalmist is gravely ill (vv.

¹⁶Because for you, O Lord, I wait;
  you, O Lord my God, will answer
¹⁷When I say, "Let them not be glad on
    my account
  who, when my foot slips, glory over
    me."

IV
¹⁸For I am very near to falling,
  and my grief is with me always.
¹⁹Indeed, I acknowledge my guilt;
  I grieve over my sin.
²⁰But my undeserved enemies are strong;
  many are my foes without cause.
²¹Those who repay evil for good
  harass me for pursuing good.
²²Forsake me not, O Lord;
  my God, be not far from me!
²³Make haste to help me,
  O Lord my salvation!

PSALM 39

The Brevity and Vanity of Life

¹For the leader, for Jeduthun. A psalm of David.

I
²I said, "I will watch my ways,
  so as not to sin with my tongue;

I will set a curb on my mouth."
While the wicked man was before me
³ I kept dumb and silent;
  I refrained from rash speech.
But my grief was stirred up;
⁴ hot grew my heart within me;
  in my thoughts, a fire blazed forth.
I spoke out with my tongue:

II
⁵Let me know, O Lord, my end
  and what is the number of my days,
  that I may learn how frail I am.
⁶A short span you have made my days,
  and my life is as nought before you;
  only a breath is any human exist-
    ence.
⁷A phantom only, man goes his ways;
  like vapor only are his restless pur-
    suits;
  he heaps up stores, and knows not
    who will use them.

III
⁸And now, for what do I wait, O Lord?
  In you is my hope.
⁹From all my sins deliver me;
  a fool's taunt let me not suffer.

4, 6-9) and recognizes that his own actions are the cause (vv. 4-5, 19) of physical and mental suffering and ostracism. There is no one to turn to for help; only the Lord can destroy the cause-and-effect chain of past folly and present misery.

Psalm 39

A mortally ill person, keenly aware of the imminent end of life, prays this individual lament (A). In verses 2-4 the psalmist resolves to remain silent, lest he speak against the God from whom all things come. The psalmist's strategy of reverent silence and submission before the all-knowing and all-effecting God has not, however, brought the hoped for healing and peace. Verses 5-7, uttered with a keen sense of the fleetingness of life, ask how long the psalmist has to live. Verses 8-10 are in tension with verses 5-7; they are a hopeful prayer for rescue after the acceptance of death. Verse 9 should read "Deliver me from all those who rise up against me," on the basis of the parallel verse. "Those who rise up" are the ones who have concluded that the illness is a punishment from God for sinful behavior and are os-

IV

¹⁰I was speechless and opened not my
   mouth,
   because it was your doing;
¹¹Take away your scourge from me;
   at the blow of your hand I wasted
   away.
¹²With rebukes for guilt you chasten
   man;
   you dissolve like a cobweb all that is
   dear to him;
   only a breath is any man.
¹³Hear my prayer, O LORD;
   to my cry give ear;
   to my weeping be not deaf!
For I am but a wayfarer before you,
   a pilgrim like all my fathers.
¹⁴Turn your gaze from me, that I may
   find respite
   ere I depart and be no more.

PSALM 40

Gratitude and Prayer for Help

¹For the leader. A psalm of David.

A

I

²I have waited, waited for the LORD,
   and he stooped toward me and
   heard my cry.
³He drew me out of the pit of destruction,

out of the mud of the swamp;
He set my feet upon a crag;
   he made firm my steps.
⁴And he put a new song into my mouth,
   a hymn to our God.
Many shall look on in awe
   and trust in the LORD.

II

⁵Happy the man who makes the LORD
   his trust;
   who turns not to idolatry
   or to those who stray after falsehood.
⁶How numerous have you made,
   O LORD, my God, your wondrous
   deeds!
And in your plans for us
   there is none to equal you;
Should I wish to declare or to tell them,
   they would be too many to recount.

III

⁷Sacrifice or oblation you wished not,
   but ears open to obedience you gave
   me.
Holocausts or sin-offerings you sought
   not;
⁸   then said I, "Behold I come;
   in the written scroll it is prescribed for
   me.
⁹To do your will, O my God, is my
   delight,

tracizing the psalmist. People judge the sick person to be punished by God
and are hurling insults.

Verse 10, recalling the resolve of silent submission of verses 2-4, is key.
The psalmist, recognizing that God is the author of all, including the mortal
illness, can only lay out the whole situation before God: "it was your doing." Verses 11-12 again reveal the tension between acceptance (v. 12) and
change (v. 11), as do verses 13-14 by the reference to Israel as guests in the
Lord's land who have no claim on the life to be found there yet have hope.

Psalm 40

Verses 2-13 are a thanksgiving (B). A distinct psalm, a lament, compris-
ing verses 14-18 has been appended, probably because it reprises some of
the vocabulary of verses 2-13. (Verses 14-18 appear also in Psalm 70 and
will be treated there.)

and your law is within my heart!"
¹⁰I announced your justice in the vast
assembly;
I did not restrain my lips, as you, O
Lord, know.
¹¹Your justice I kept not hid within my
heart;
your faithfulness and your salvation
I have spoken of;
I have made no secret of your kindness
and your truth
in the vast assembly.

B

I

¹²Withhold not, O Lord, your compassion from me;
may your kindness and your truth
ever preserve me.
¹³For all about me are evils beyond
reckoning;
my sins so overcome me that I cannot see;
They are more numerous than the hairs
of my head,
and my heart fails me.

II

¹⁴Deign, O Lord, to rescue me;
O Lord, make haste to help me.
¹⁵Let all be put to shame and confusion
who seek to snatch away my life.
Let them be turned back in disgrace
who desire my ruin.
¹⁶Let them be dismayed in their shame
who say to me, "Aha, aha!"
¹⁷But may all who seek you
exult and be glad in you,
And may those who love your salvation
say ever, "The Lord be glorified."
¹⁸Though I am afflicted and poor,
yet the Lord thinks of me.
You are my help and my deliverer;
O my God, hold not back!

PSALM 41
Thanksgiving after Sickness

¹For the leader. A psalm of David.

I

²Happy is he who has regard for the
lowly and the poor;
in the day of misfortune the Lord will
deliver him.

The psalmist describes God's rescue in spatial terms, as the pulling out
of someone trapped in a bog onto dry land. Even in adversity he hoped.
Verse 4 states that rendering thanks is not simply a gift one makes to the
Lord in return for rescue but is itself a gift of God. It makes visible to one's
neighbors the divine act of mercy (v. 4b). The next verse associates the individual salvation with the great acts of salvation of Israel's past.

Verses 7-9 have suffered some displacement but the gist is clear: the rescued person was expected to offer sacrifice but declares that God desires obedience instead. The verse recalls the memorable words of Samuel to Saul
in 1 Sam 15:22: "Obedience is better than sacrifice, and submission than the
fat of rams." The mysterious "Behold I come" in verse 8 may reflect a scene
like that of Ps 118:19, "Open to me the gates of justice; I will enter them
and give thanks to the Lord." The psalmist, then, would enter the temple
precincts to give thanks, not with the sacrifice of animals, but with a new
song and a devotion to "your law." The final verses emphasize the unre-
strained, open-hearted proclamation that characterizes one who has experienced the saving mercy of God.

³The Lord will keep and preserve him;
 he will make him happy on the
  earth,
and not give him over to the will of
 his enemies.
⁴The Lord will help him on his sickbed,
 he will take away all his ailment
  when he is ill.

II

⁵Once I said, "O Lord, have pity on me;
 heal me, though I have sinned against
  you.
⁶My enemies say the worst of me:
 'When will he die and his name perish?'
⁷When one comes to see me, he speaks
 without sincerity;
 his heart stores up malice;
 when he leaves he gives voice to it
  outside.
⁸ All my foes whisper together against
  me;

against me they imagine the worst:
⁹'A malignant disease fills his frame';
 and 'Now that he lies ill, he will not
  rise again.'
¹⁰Even my friend who had my trust
 and partook of my bread, has raised
  his heel against me.   (III)
¹¹But you, O Lord, have pity on me, and
  raise me up,
 that I may repay them."
¹²That you love me I know by this,
 that my enemy does not triumph over
  me,
¹³But because of my integrity you sustain me
 and let me stand before you forever.

*   *   *

¹⁴Blessed be the Lord, the God of Israel,
 from all eternity and forever. Amen.
  Amen.

Psalm 41

This psalm of thanksgiving (B) recounts God's rescue of a sick individual (vv. 4, 5, and 9). The psalmist begins by declaring blessed, that is, regarded favorably by God, those who behave well toward the poor (v. 2). Other psalms use the same formula for those who have been placed in a right relation to God (Pss 32:1-2; 34:9; 40:5; 65:5), but here the right relation is toward the special friends of the Lord.

The psalmist has apparently become part of that privileged group who have experienced the Lord's protection (vv. 3-4), sometimes called "the poor" in the Bible. The narrative of the rescue, essential to a thanksgiving, is done in this psalm by quoting the psalmist's lament before rescue (vv. 5-11). Verse 5 is the beginning of the prayer, "Once I said . . . ." The misery of the past contrasts with present safety. The quoted prayer shows that the chief pain was not physical but emotional—betrayal by enemies, among whom were friends. They wanted all memory of the sufferer erased (a horrible fate for the Hebrew) because they judged the affliction to be the fruit of sin. By their talk they encouraged the separation of the sufferer from the community of God.

Verse 11, the petition for health to requite the enemies, is disturbing to modern readers; the point is that the healing itself is an act of judgment through which God decides for the defendant and against the false friends.

II: THE SECOND BOOK—Psalms 42–72

PSALM 42
Desire for God and His Temple

¹For the leader. A *maskil* of the sons of Korah.

I

²As the hind longs for the running
waters,
so my soul longs for you, O God.
³Athirst is my soul for God, the living
God.
When shall I go and behold the face of
God?
⁴My tears are my food day and night,
as they say to me day after day,
"Where is your God?"
⁵Those times I recall,
now that I pour out my soul within
me,
When I went with the throng
and led them in procession to the
house of God,
Amid loud cries of joy and thanksgiving,
with the multitude keeping festival.

⁶ Why are you so downcast, O my
soul?
Why do you sigh within me?
Hope in God! For I shall again
be thanking him,
in the presence of my savior
and my God.

II

⁷Within me my soul is downcast;
so will I remember you
From the land of the Jordan and of
Hermon,
from Mount Mizar.
⁸Deep calls unto deep
in the roar of your cataracts;
All your breakers and your billows
pass over me.
⁹By day the LORD bestows his grace,
and at night I have his song,
a prayer to my living God.
¹⁰I sing to God, my rock:
"Why do you forget me?
Why must I go about in mourning,
with the enemy oppressing me?"
¹¹It crushes my bones that my foes mock
me,

The judicial tone carries over to verses 12-13: recovery from illness is a mark of favor showing God's love for this individual. The integrity of which the psalmist boasts is his innocence in the present situation, not for the totality of his life. The blessing in verse 14 is not part of the psalm; it marks the end of Book I, the so-called collection of David's psalms.

BOOK II: PSALMS 42–72

Psalms 42–43

The refrain "Why are you so downcast, O my soul," repeated in 42:6, 12, and 43:5, shows that Psalms 42–43 are a single poem; the traditional separation into two psalms is wrong. It is a lament (A) of an individual who lives beyond Israel's borders in the north and who longs to join the community of God worshiping in the temple in Jerusalem. In the Hebrew scriptures Yahweh is the God of all the world but is revealed only in Jerusalem. What distresses the psalmist is the absence of God, the feeling of deep hunger without the ability to satisfy it because of distance from Jerusalem and the hindrance of enemies. Their taunt, "Where is your God?" (vv. 4, 11), intensifies the pain.

as they say to me day after day,
"Where is your God?"
12 Why are you so downcast, O my
soul?
Why do you sigh within me?
Hope in God! For I shall again be
thanking him,
in the presence of my savior
and my God.

PSALM 43

III
¹Do me justice, O God, and fight my
fight
against a faithless people;
from the deceitful and impious man
rescue me.
²For you, O God, are my strength.
Why do you keep me so far away?
Why must I go about in mourning,
with the enemy oppressing me?
³Send forth your light and your fidelity;
they shall lead me on
And bring me to your holy mountain,
to your dwelling-place.
⁴Then will I go in to the altar of God,
the God of my gladness and joy;
Then will I give you thanks upon the
harp,

O God, my God!
5 Why are you so downcast, O my
soul?
Why do you sigh within me?
Hope in God! For I shall again be
thanking him,
in the presence of my savior and
my God.

PSALM 44

Israel's Past Glory and Present Need

¹For the leader. A *maskil* of the sons of Korah.
I
²O God, our ears have heard,
our fathers have declared to us,
The deeds you did in their days,
in days of old:
³How with your own hand you rooted
out the nations and planted them;
you smashed the peoples, but for
them you made room.
⁴For not with their own sword did they
conquer the land,
nor did their own arm make them
victorious,
But it was your arm and your right hand
and the light of your countenance,
in your love for them.

Verses 7-8 show that the psalmist is in the north; Mount Mizar is generally thought to be a mountain in the region of Mount Hermon. In verse 9
the psalmist is caught like Jonah (Jonah 2:3-4) in the deep, a metaphor for
the place where Yahweh will not be found. In the last of the three stanzas,
Ps 43:1-5, the psalmist prays that Yahweh decide against the enemies who
say that Yahweh cannot bring the psalmist to Jerusalem.

Psalm 44

Community laments (A) are often built on the contrast between God's
gracious creation of Israel through the Exodus-Conquest and the present distress that seems to negate that creation. The Lord expelled the nations in
order to give Israel its land (vv. 2-9), but now the nations expel Israel from
that land (vv. 10-17), undoing God's work. Verses 2-9 emphasize the divine
initiative in the grant of the land. Israel does nothing—everything is done
because of God's own gracious will. But the Lord is now silent as the people

⁵You are my king and my God,
  who bestowed victories on Jacob.
⁶Our foes through you we struck down;
  through your name we trampled
    down our adversaries.
⁷For not in my bow did I trust,
  nor did my sword save me;
⁸But you saved us from our foes,
  and those who hated us you put to
    shame.
⁹In God we gloried day by day;
  your name we praised always.

  II
¹⁰Yet now you have cast us off and put us
    in disgrace,
  and you go not forth with our armies.
¹¹You have let us be driven back by our
    foes;
  those who hated us plundered us at
    will.
¹²You marked us out as sheep to be
    slaughtered;
  among the nations you scattered us.
¹³You sold your people for no great
    price;
  you made no profit from the sale of
    them.
¹⁴You made us the reproach of our
    neighbors,
  the mockery and the scorn of those
    around us.
¹⁵You made us a byword among the
    nations,
  a laughingstock among the peoples.
¹⁶All the day my disgrace is before me,
  and shame covers my face
¹⁷At the voice of him who mocks and
    blasphemes,
  and in the presence of the enemy and
    the avenger.

  III
¹⁸All this has come upon us, though we
    have not forgotten you,
  nor have we been disloyal to your
    covenant;
¹⁹Our hearts have not shrunk back,
  nor our steps turned aside from your
    path,
²⁰Though you thrust us down into a
    place of misery
  and covered us over with darkness.
²¹If we had forgotten the name of our
    God
  and stretched out our hands to a
    strange god,
²²Would not God have discovered this?
  For he knows the secrets of the heart.
²³Yet for your sake we are being slain
    all the day;
  we are looked upon as sheep to be
    slaughtered.

  IV
²⁴Awake! Why are you asleep, O Lᴏʀᴅ?
  Arise! Cast us not off forever!
²⁵Why do you hide your face,
  forgetting our woe and our oppres-
    sion?
²⁶For our souls are bowed down to the
    dust,
  our bodies are pressed to the earth.
²⁷Arise, help us!
  Redeem us for your kindness' sake.

PSALM 45

Nuptial Ode for the Messianic King

¹For the leader; according to "Lilies." A *maskil* of
the sons of Korah. A love song.

  I
²My heart overflows with a goodly
    theme;

are despoiled, even though they are not conscious of any sin against the covenant (vv. 18-23). Here the community struggles with being the Lord's special people and witness while the Lord remains silent before their real pain.
Keenly aware of the divine favor that gave them the land in the past, they
wait for God's return. The last three verses are a spirited prayer for help,
showing that the people do not lose hope.

as I sing my ode to the king,
  my tongue is nimble as the pen of a
  skillful scribe.

II

³Fairer in beauty are you than the sons
  of men;
  grace is poured out upon your lips;
  thus God has blessed you forever.
⁴Gird your sword upon your thigh, O
  mighty one!
  In your splendor and your majesty
  ride on triumphant
⁵In the cause of truth and for the sake
  of justice;
  and may your right hand show you
  wondrous deeds.
⁶Your arrows are sharp; peoples are subject to you;
  the king's enemies lose heart.
⁷Your throne, O God, stands forever and
  ever;
  a tempered rod is your royal scepter.
⁸You love justice and hate wickedness;
  therefore God, your God, has
  anointed you
  with the oil of gladness above your
  fellow kings.
⁹With myrrh and aloes and cassia your
  robes are fragrant;
  from ivory palaces string music brings
  you joy.

¹⁰The daughters of kings come to meet
  you;
  the queen takes her place at your
  right hand in gold of Ophir.

III

¹¹Hear, O daughter, and see; turn your
  ear,
  forget your people and your father's
  house.
¹²So shall the king desire your beauty;
  for he is your lord, and you must
  worship him.
¹³And the city of Tyre is here with gifts;
  the rich among the people seek your
  favor.
¹⁴All glorious is the king's daughter as
  she enters;
  her raiment is threaded with spun
  gold.
¹⁵In embroidered apparel she is borne in
  to the king;
  behind her the virgins of her train are
  brought to you.
¹⁶They are borne in with gladness and
  joy;
  they enter the palace of the king.

IV

¹⁷The place of your fathers your sons shall
  have;
  you shall make them princes through
  all the land.

Psalm 45

This poem is perhaps the most specific in the Psalter; it was sung at the king's marriage to a princess of Phoenicia. Retained in the collection when there was no reigning king, it came to be applied to the anointed king who was to come, the Messiah.

The court poet, conscious of the power of his song (vv. 2, 18), sings first of the Lord's choice of the king over others (vv. 3, 8bc) and of his privilege of establishing the Lord's purpose (vv. 4-8). In verse 9 the poet depicts the ceremony in which the bride, in a majestic procession, is led to the king. The princess is to forget the royal house she came from ("your father's house" of verse 11) and be wife to the king, the viceroy of the Lord of all the earth. Verse 17 is addressed to the king; with his new wife the ancient Davidic (and Abrahamic) promise of progeny and power will come true.

¹⁸I will make your name memorable
through all generations;
therefore shall nations praise you
forever and ever.

PSALM 46
God the Refuge of Israel

¹For the leader. A song of the sons of Korah; according to "Virgins."

I

²God is our refuge and our strength,
an ever-present help in distress.
³Therefore we fear not, though the earth
be shaken
and mountains plunge into the depths
of the sea;
⁴Though its waters rage and foam
and the mountains quake at its
surging.
The LORD of hosts is with us;
our stronghold is the God of
Jacob.

II

⁵There is a stream whose runlets gladden the city of God,
the holy dwelling of the Most High.

⁶God is in its midst; it shall not be disturbed;
God will help it at the break of dawn.

⁷Though nations are in turmoil, kingdoms totter,
his voice resounds, the earth melts
away,
⁸   The LORD of hosts is with us;
our stronghold is the God of
Jacob.

III

⁹Come! behold the deeds of the LORD,
the astounding things he has wrought
on earth:
¹⁰He has stopped wars to the end of the
earth:
the bow he breaks; he splinters the
spears;
he burns the shields with fire.
¹¹Desist! and confess that I am God,
exalted among the nations, exalted
upon the earth.
¹²   The LORD of hosts is with us;
our stronghold is the God of
Jacob.

Psalm 46

In this song of Zion, Yahweh is hymned for making the holy city a sure refuge to worshipers, who are terrified by the prospect of a collapsing world. There are three stanzas (vv. 2-4, vv. 5-8, vv. 9-12); the last two are ended by the refrain of verses 8 and 12.

God created the world by subduing the disorderly primal forces that made human life impossible, and established Zion as the glorious divine dwelling. Because God is present at the ordered world's center, the psalmist is confident that there will be no unleashing of those once unruly forces (vv. 2-4), especially in the Lord's own space. The city and temple of the Lord are the place where the memory of God's creation victory is most vivid. That creation can be celebrated in the Lord's shrine, even though the nations, unruly like the primal forces, rage outside (vv. 5-8). The very buildings of the city make visible to the chosen community how powerful the Lord is over all that is chaotic and anti-human. Verse 11 majestically commands all hateful and hurtful powers to submit to the Lord.

PSALM 47

The Lord the King of All Nations

[1]For the leader. A psalm of the sons of Korah.

I

[2]All you peoples, clap your hands,
shout to God with cries of gladness,
[3]For the LORD, the Most High, the awesome,
is the great king over all the earth.
[4]He brings peoples under us;
nations under our feet.
[5]He chooses for us our inheritance,
the glory of Jacob, whom he loves.

II

[6]God mounts his throne amid shouts of joy;
the LORD, amid trumpet blasts.
[7]Sing praise to God, sing praise;
sing praise to our king, sing praise.

III

[8]For king of all the earth is God;
sing hymns of praise.
[9]God reigns over the nations,
God sits upon his holy throne.
[10]The princes of the peoples are gathered together

with the people of the God of Abraham.
For God's are the guardians of the earth;
he is supreme.

PSALM 48

Thanksgiving for Jerusalem's Deliverance

[1]A psalm of the sons of Korah; a song.

I

[2]Great is the LORD and wholly to be praised
in the city of our God.
His holy mountain, [3]fairest of heights,
is the joy of all the earth;
Mount Zion, "the recesses of the North,"
is the city of the great King.
[4]God is with her castles;
renowned is he as a stronghold.

II

[5]For lo! the kings assemble,
they come on together;
[6]They also see, and at once are stunned,
terrified, routed;

Psalm 47

This enthronement psalm celebrates the kingship of Yahweh over all the beings of heaven and earth. The Lord, invisibly enthroned upon the ark is carried in procession into the temple.

The psalm is divided into two parts of equal length, verses 2-6 and 7-10, each beginning with a call to praise. The thought expressed in each stanza is the same: Yahweh is the king, victorious over the powers of heaven and earth (the powers of earth are emphasized in this psalm), and selects Israel as a special people (vv. 5 and 10). The choice of Israel is part of the establishment of the world. Verse 6 probably refers to the trumpet blasts and shouts that accompanied the entry of the ark into the temple, the entry signifying Yahweh's taking possession of the temple as king.

Psalm 48

This psalm praises Zion, the city where Yahweh's world-establishing victory is remembered. The splendid buildings, especially the temple, bespeak Yahweh's power to protect the people from all attack. So suffused with Yah-

⁷Quaking seizes them there;
  anguish, like a woman's in labor,
⁸As though a wind from the east
  were shattering ships of Tarshish.

III

⁹As we had heard, so have we seen
  in the city of the LORD of hosts,
In the city of our God;
  God makes it firm forever.
¹⁰O God, we ponder your kindness
  within your temple.
¹¹As your name, O God, so also your
  praise
  reaches to the ends of the earth.
Of justice your right hand is full;
¹² let Mount Zion be glad,
Let the cities of Judah rejoice,
  because of your judgments.

IV

¹³Go about Zion, make the round;
  count her towers.

¹⁴Consider her ramparts,
  examine her castles,
That you may tell a future generation
¹⁵ that such is God,
Our God forever and ever;
  he will guide us.

PSALM 49

The Vanity of Worldly Riches

¹For the leader. A psalm of the sons of Korah.
²Hear this, all you peoples;
  hearken, all who dwell in the world,
³Of lowly birth or high degree,
  rich and poor alike.
⁴My mouth shall speak wisdom;
  prudence shall be the utterance of my
  heart.
⁵My ear is intent upon a proverb;
  I will set forth my riddle to the music
  of the harp.

weh's presence is the site of the holy mountain that the psalmist declares the mountain to be higher and more beautiful than any other and to be impregnable to all enemies.

Verses 2-3 praise the mountain where God graciously encounters human beings. The next section, verses 4-9, describes the great deed that proved the Lord's presence on the mountain: the easy defeat of the enemy kings by means of God's storm wind. Verses 10-12 describe the festivities of triumph, resounding far and wide in celebration of the victory that establishes the world. "We ponder" (v. 10) means "we recite" (the stories of Yahweh's victories). The final part, verses 13-15, sees in the solid structures of the temple and city such clear evidence of divine might and loving protection that one need only walk through them to feel secure and loved.

Psalm 49

Though often called a "wisdom psalm" because it contains reflections about the human condition, Psalm 49 is really a confession of trust in God like Ps 27:1-6, except that here there is a more confident tone (note the assurance of vv. 2-5). Also, the enemy is seen in greater profundity—it is death itself.

The opening verses, like Ps 78:1-4, boldly make a new statement about human life before God. In verses 6-10 the psalmist refuses to fear the wealthy who are wicked; their wealth cannot protect them from the ultimate enemy,

I

⁶Why should I fear in evil days
　when my wicked ensnarers ring me
　round?
⁷They trust in their wealth;
　the abundance of their riches is their
　boast.
⁸Yet in no way can a man redeem him-
　self,
　or pay his own ransom to God;
⁹Too high is the price to redeem one's
　life; he would never have enough
10　to remain alive always and not see
　destruction.
¹¹For he can see that wise men die,
　and likewise the senseless and the
　stupid pass away,
　leaving to others their wealth.
¹²Tombs are their homes forever,
　their dwellings through all genera-
　tions,
　though they have called lands by their
　names.
13　Thus man, for all his splendor,
　does not abide;
　he resembles the beasts that
　perish.

II

¹⁴This is the way of those whose trust is
　folly,

the end of those contented with their
　lot:
¹⁵Like sheep they are herded into the
　nether world;
　death is their shepherd, and the up-
　right rule over them.
Quickly their form is consumed;
　the nether world is their palace.
¹⁶But God will redeem me
　from the power of the nether world
　by receiving me.

III

¹⁷Fear not when a man grows rich,
　when the wealth of his house be-
　comes great,
¹⁸For when he dies, he shall take none of
　it;
　his wealth shall not follow him
　down.
¹⁹Though in his lifetime he counted him-
　self blessed,
　"They will praise you for doing well
　for yourself,"
²⁰He shall join the circle of his fore-
　bears
　who shall never more see light.
21　Man, for all his splendor, if he
　have not prudence,
　resembles the beasts that per-
　ish.

death. Experience shows that death takes all, the wise (=the righteous) and the wicked. The wealth that once emboldened the wicked to do violence will be scattered. A refrain stating that death levels all closes the first part in verse 13, as it will the second part in verse 21. Verses 14-15 emphasize the theme of the first part: those who live by wealth and violence somehow have death as their shepherd. In contrast, the innocent afflicted person who refuses to fear (v. 6) has as shepherd Yahweh, who will in a mysterious way protect that trusting person from death. The perhaps deliberately enigmatic "by receiving me" recalls God's taking of Enoch in Gen 5:24 (compare 2 Kgs 2:11-12). The Hebrew of verse 16 sounds like and plays on verse 9: a human cannot ransom or save another human but God can save "me," the trusting or persecuted person. In verses 17-21 the psalmist exhorts from the conviction that human beings are not to be feared—they will all die. Only God is the ultimate ransomer.

PSALM 50
The Acceptable Sacrifice

¹A psalm of Asaph.

I

God the LORD has spoken and summoned the earth,
from the rising of the sun to its set-
ting.
²From Zion, perfect in beauty,
God shines forth.
³May our God come and not be deaf to
us!
Before him is a devouring fire;
around him is a raging storm.
⁴He summons the heavens from above,
and the earth, to the trial of his
people:
⁵"Gather my faithful ones before me,
those who have made a covenant
with me by sacrifice."
⁶And the heavens proclaim his justice;
for God himself is the judge.

II

⁷"Hear, my people, and I will speak;
Israel, I will testify against you;
God, your God, am I.
⁸Not for your sacrifices do I rebuke you,
for your holocausts are before me
always.

⁹I take from your house no bullock,
no goats out of your fold.
¹⁰For mine are all the animals of the
forests,
beasts by the thousand on my mountains.
¹¹I know all the birds of the air,
and whatever stirs in the plains, belongs to me.
¹²If I were hungry, I should not tell you,
for mine are the world and its fullness.
¹³Do I eat the flesh of strong bulls,
or is the blood of goats my drink?
¹⁴Offer to God praise as your sacrifice
and fulfill your vows to the Most
High;
¹⁵Then call upon me in time of distress;
I will rescue you, and you shall
glorify me."

III

¹⁶But to the wicked man God says:
"Why do you recite my statutes,
and profess my covenant with your
mouth,
¹⁷Though you hate discipline
and cast my words behind you?
¹⁸When you see a thief, you keep pace
with him,

Psalm 50

Psalm 50 is the record of a ceremony in which the Lord judges the people gathered on Mount Zion. Have they been faithful to the covenant, positively by worshiping and calling upon the Lord alone (as opposed to false gods, vv. 14-15), negatively by avoiding violations of the Ten Commandments (vv. 16-20)? Only a selection of the basic commandments are listed in the psalm. The liturgy reenacts the great encounter of the Lord and Israel at Sinai (Exod 19–24). In liturgical time Mount Zion stands for Mount Sinai as each generation of Israel faces the Lord.

Verses 1-6 describe the manifestation of the Lord on Mount Zion, medi-ated, in all probability, through trumpet blasts and smoke and fire. In verse 6 the heavens are summoned as witnesses to the people's conduct; heaven and earth (and other cosmic pairs) were often invoked in antiquity as wit-nesses at the sealing of covenants. Verses 7-15 are divine speech, mediated

and with adulterers you throw in
your lot.
¹⁹To your mouth you give free rein for
evil,
you harness your tongue to deceit.
²⁰You sit speaking against your brother;
against your mother's son you spread
rumors.
²¹When you do these things, shall I be
deaf to it?
Or do you think that I am like yourself?
I will correct you by drawing them up
before your eyes.

IV
²²"Consider this, you who forget God,
lest I rend you and there be no one to
rescue you.
²³He that offers praise as a sacrifice
glorifies me;
and to him that goes the right way I
will show the salvation of God."

PSALM 51
The Miserere: Prayer of Repentance

¹For the leader. A psalm of David, ²when Nathan
the prophet came to him after his sin with Bathsheba.

A

³Have mercy on me, O God, in your
goodness;
in the greatness of your compassion
wipe out my offense.
⁴Thoroughly wash me from my guilt
and of my sin cleanse me.

B

I
⁵For I acknowledge my offense,
and my sin is before me always:
⁶"Against you only have I sinned,
and done what is evil in your sight"—
That you may be justified in your sentence,
vindicated when you condemn.
⁷Indeed, in guilt was I born,

by the voice of the priest; the Lord does not need the food of animal sacrifice
as do the gods of the ancient world (vv. 8-17) but desires the freely given
response of the people (vv. 14-15). In verses 16-21 that same divine voice
judges the wicked, that is, those who violate the fundamental covenant rela-
tionship. Such people are to repent, change. Verses 22-23, despite their vigor,
are a positive conclusion to the liturgical encounter: the Lord seeks the free
response of the people.

Psalm 51
One of the great laments (A) in the Psalter, this Penitential Psalm (see
p. 11) is primarily a plea for the removal of the personal and social distress that sins have caused. The poem is divided into two parts of approximately equal length: verses 3-10 and 11-19, with a coda in vv. 20-21. The
two parts are carefully interlocked by repetition of significant words: "blot
(wipe) out" in the first verse of each section (vv. 3 and 11); "wash me" in
the verse just after the first verse of the first section (v. 4) and just before
the last verse (v. 9) of the first section; the repetition of "heart," "God," and
"spirit" in verses 12 and 19.

In the first section the psalmist, relying entirely on God's gracious fidelity, prays to be delivered from sin. Verse 10 suggests that the psalmist is sick,
and attributes the sickness to sin. Sin is depicted with intense realism, not

and in sin my mother conceived me;
⁸Behold, you are pleased with sincerity of heart,
and in my inmost being you teach me wisdom.

II
⁹Cleanse me of sin with hyssop, that I may be purified;
wash me, and I shall be whiter than snow.
¹⁰Let me hear the sounds of joy and gladness;
the bones you have crushed shall rejoice.
¹¹Turn away your face from my sins,
and blot out all my guilt.

III
¹²A clean heart create for me, O God,
and a steadfast spirit renew within me.
¹³Cast me not out from your presence,
and your holy spirit take not from me.
¹⁴Give me back the joy of your salvation,
and a willing spirit sustain in me.

IV
¹⁵I will teach transgressors your ways,
and sinners shall return to you.
¹⁶Free me from blood guilt, O God, my saving God;
then my tongue shall revel in your justice.
¹⁷O Lord, open my lips,
and my mouth shall proclaim your praise.
¹⁸For you are not pleased with sacrifices;
should I offer a holocaust, you would not accept it.
¹⁹My sacrifice, O God, is a contrite spirit;
a heart contrite and humbled, O God, you will not spurn.

C
²⁰Be bountiful, O LORD, to Zion in your kindness
by rebuilding the walls of Jerusalem;
²¹Then shall you be pleased with due sacrifices,
burnt offerings and holocausts;
then shall they offer up bullocks on your altar.

just a past act against God but its emotional, physical, and social consequences. The psalmist experiences the destructive results of sin (v. 5) and knows that this suffering is self-inflicted and deserved. Before the all-holy God a human being can plead no self-righteousness (v. 7) but can only ask for God's purifying favor (vv. 8-10).

Verse 11 begins the second part by repeating the prayer for forgiveness. Something more profound than the wiping clean of sin is the theme of verses 12-19, namely, a state of nearness to God, a living by the spirit or power of God (vv. 12-13). Such nearness brings joy (v. 14) and enables the forgiven sinner to speak from personal experience to all who are estranged from God (vv. 15-16). That proclamation is the response that God desires, even more than sacrifice in the temple (vv. 17-19). The last two verses make precise the situation: the experience of sin is the exilic absence of God from the temple and its ceremonies.

Psalm 52

Though often classed as a lament, this psalm is unique. The psalmist pronounces judgment upon the wealthy and self-sufficient violent person

PSALM 52
The Deceitful Tongue

[1]For the leader. A *maskil* of David, [2]when Doeg the Edomite went and told Saul, "David went to the house of Ahimelech."

I

[3]Why do you glory in evil,
  you champion of infamy?
All the day [4]you plot harm;
  your tongue is like a sharpened razor,
  you practiced deceiver!
[5]You love evil rather than good,
  falsehood rather than honest speech.
[6]You love all that means ruin,
  you of the deceitful tongue!

II

[7]God himself shall demolish you;
  forever he shall break you;
He shall pluck you from your tent,
  and uproot you from the land of the living.

III

[8]The just shall look on with awe;
  then they shall laugh at him:

[9]"This is the man who made not
  God the source of his strength,
But put his trust in his great wealth,
  and his strength in harmful plots."
[10]But I, like a green olive tree
  in the house of God,
Trust in the kindness of God
  forever and ever.
[11]I will thank you always for what you
  have done,
  and proclaim the goodness of your
  name
  before your faithful ones.

PSALM 53
Lament over Widespread Corruption

[1]For the leader; according to *Mahalath*. A *maskil* of David.

I

[2]The fool says in his heart,
  "There is no God."
Such are corrupt; they do abominable
  deeds;
  there is not one who does good.

whose prosperity is a temptation to "the godly," that is, those loyal to God in all things. One can compare Isa 22:15-18, in which the prophet denounces Shebna, a royal official, for his arrogance.

Verses 3-6 resemble a prophetic accusation against the arrogant. The speaker is one of the righteous: in the psalms they often are the victims of "champions of infamy." Lies, violence, and exploitation are their way of life; their prosperity tempts those who believe that God rewards only the righteous. The cry for judgment in verse 7 comes from the troubled heart of a righteous person who believes that the Lord will not allow the godless to triumph. The removal of the godless from the land of the living assures the righteous that the just God is active in their regard; the divine act makes them rejoice (vv. 8-9). Rejoicing over a fallen enemy is distasteful to modern readers, as are the neat categories "the righteous" and "the worker of treachery." The psalmist, however, is not speaking of permanent categories of being but only of the present unfair situation. The psalmist presumably would not deny that a righteous person could join the ranks of the wicked tomorrow, or vice versa.

The last verses are full of confidence. Nearness to God is the ultimate answer to the experience of injustice. Olive trees grow in the sacred precincts

³God looks down from heaven upon the children of men
> to see if there be one who is wise and seeks God.

⁴All alike have gone astray; they have become perverse;
> there is not one who does good, not even one.

II

⁵Will all these evildoers never learn,
> they who eat up my people just as they eat bread,
> who call not upon God?

⁶There they were in great fear, where no fear was,
> For God has scattered the bones of your besiegers;
> they are put to shame, because God has rejected them.

III

⁷Oh, that out of Zion would come the salvation of Israel!
> When God restores the well-being of his people,
> then shall Jacob exult and Israel be glad.

PSALM 54
Confident Prayer in Great Peril

¹For the leader; with stringed instruments. A *maskil* of David, ²when the Ziphites went and said to Saul, "David is hiding among us."

I

³O God, by your name save me,
> and by your might defend my cause.

⁴O God, hear my prayer;
> hearken to the words of my mouth.

⁵For haughty men have risen up against me,
> and fierce men seek my life;
> they set not God before their eyes.

II

⁶Behold, God is my helper;
> the Lord sustains my life.

⁷Turn back the evil upon my foes;
> in your faithfulness destroy them.

⁸Freely will I offer you sacrifice;
> I will praise your name, O Lᴏʀᴅ, for its goodness,

⁹Because from all distress you have rescued me,
> and my eyes look down upon my enemies.

of the Dome of the Rock in Jerusalem even today, their fertility testifying to God's presence in the shrine. The last verses thank God for upholding justice; the godly can rejoice in divine protection.

Psalm 53

Psalm 53 duplicates Psalm 14, where commentary is given (see p. 18).

Psalm 54

The psalm is almost a textbook lament (A). The troubled person, attacked by the wicked, calls upon Yahweh directly for help (vv. 3-5). The psalmist refuses to despair and hopes in God, who is active in human history and is just (vv. 6-7). Verses 8-9 render thanks with a certitude that suggests that a priest has in the meantime spoken a reassuring oracle (not transmitted) and the psalmist has accepted it as the word of the God who has promised protection to the poor.

PSALM 55

Complaint against Enemies and a Disloyal Companion

[1]For the leader; with stringed instruments. A *maskil* of David.

I

[2]Hearken, O God, to my prayer;
turn not away from my pleading;
[3] give heed to me, and answer me.
I rock with grief, and am troubled
[4] at the voice of the enemy and the clamor of the wicked.
For they bring down evil upon me,
and with fury they persecute me.
[5]My heart quakes within me;
the terror of death has fallen upon me.
[6]Fear and trembling come upon me,
and horror overwhelms me,
[7]And I say, "Had I but wings like a dove,
I would fly away and be at rest.
[8]Far away I would flee;
I would lodge in the wilderness.
[9]I would hasten to find shelter
from the violent storm and the tempest."

II

[10]Engulf them, O Lord; divide their counsels,
for in the city I see violence and strife;
[11] day and night they prowl about upon its walls.

Evil and mischief are in its midst;
[12] [treachery is in its midst;]
oppression and fraud never depart from its streets.
[13]If an enemy had reviled me,
I could have borne it;
If he who hates me had vaunted himself against me,
I might have hidden from him.
[14]But you, my other self,
my companion and my bosom friend!
[15]You, whose comradeship I enjoyed;
at whose side I walked in procession in the house of God!

III

[16]Let death surprise them;
let them go down alive to the nether world,
for evil is in their dwellings, in their very midst.
[17]But I will call upon God,
and the LORD will save me.
[18]In the evening, and at dawn, and at noon,
I will grieve and moan,
and he will hear my voice.
[19]He will give me freedom and peace
from those who war against me,
for many there are who oppose me.
[20]God will hear me and will humble them
from his eternal throne;
For improvement is not in them,
nor do they fear God.
[21]Each one lays hands on his associates,
and violates his pact.

Psalm 55

The psalmist, betrayed by those who were once intimate friends (vv. 14-15 and 21-22), prays that God punish those oath breakers and thus be recognized as the protector of the wronged. The customary structure of the lament (A) is verified here: the unadorned address to God (v. 2); the prayer for deliverance and punishment of the enemy (vv. 3, 10, 16); the vivid dramatization of the oppressive situation so as to appeal to God's sense of honor (vv. 4-9, 11-15, 21-22). The malice of the personal enemy is seen by the psalmist as an instance of the mysterious residual evil in the world, an evil that is palpable in the streets of the city (vv. 11-12). It frightens and dis-

²²Softer than butter is his speech,
  but war is in his heart;
His words are smoother than oil,
  but they are drawn swords.
²³Cast your care upon the LORD,
  and he will support you;
  never will he permit the just man to
  be disturbed.
²⁴And you, O God, will bring them
  down
  into the pit of destruction;
Men of blood and deceit shall not live
  out half their days.
  But I trust in you, O LORD.

PSALM 56

Trust in God, the Helper in Need

¹For the leader; according to *Jonath . . . rehokim.*
A *miktam* of David, when the Philistines held him
in Gath.

I

²Have pity on me, O God, for men
  trample upon me;
  all the day they press their attack
  against me.
³My adversaries trample upon me all the
  day;
  yes, many fight against me.
O Most High, ⁴when I begin to fear,
  in you will I trust.
⁵   In God, in whose promise I glory,

in God I trust without fear;
  what can flesh do against me?

II

⁶All the day they molest me in my
  efforts;
  their every thought is of evil against
  me.
⁷They gather together in hiding,
  they watch my steps.
As they have waited for my life,
⁸ because of their wickedness keep
  them in view:
  in your wrath bring down the
  peoples, O God.
⁹My wanderings you have counted;
  my tears are stored in your flask;
  are they not recorded in your book?
¹⁰Then do my enemies turn back,
  when I call upon you;
  now I know that God is with me.
¹¹   In God, in whose promise I glory,
¹²   in God I trust without fear;
  what can flesh do against me?

III

¹³I am bound, O God, by vows to you;
  your thank offerings I will fulfill.
¹⁴For you have rescued me from death,
  my feet, too, from stumbling;
  that I may walk before God in the
  light of the living.

courages those who trust in the Lord. As in other laments, the psalmist trusts so strongly in the salvation of God that he can exhort others (v. 23) and live calmly in the expectation of salvation (v. 24).

Psalm 56

The lament (A) of a person whose enemies threaten death (v. 14) but cannot ultimately keep him from uttering a prayer of trust is enclosed by a refrain (vv. 4-5 and 11-12). The psalmist is glad to be one of the poor, the *'anawim*, who by their vulnerability to the attacks of the powerful and wicked invite the special protection of the just and merciful Lord (vv. 2-3). So sure is the hope of the poor that they need not fear even at the height of danger (vv. 4-5 and 11-12). At the moment of danger, which the psalmist does not minimize (vv. 2-8), they can be certain that God tenderly regards their tears

PSALM 57

Confident Prayer for Deliverance

¹For the leader. (Do not destroy!) A *miktam* of David, when he fled away from Saul into the cave.

I

²Have pity on me, O God; have pity on me,
for in you I take refuge.
In the shadow of your wings I take refuge,
till harm pass by.
³I call to God the Most High,
to God, my benefactor.
⁴May he send from heaven and save me;
may he make those a reproach who trample upon me;
may God send his kindness and his faithfulness.
⁵I lie prostrate in the midst of lions
which devour men;
Their teeth are spears and arrows,
their tongue is a sharp sword.
⁶ Be exalted above the heavens, O God;
above all the earth be your glory!

II

⁷They have prepared a net for my feet;
they have bowed me down;
They have dug a pit before me,
but they fall into it.
⁸My heart is steadfast, O God; my heart is steadfast;
I will sing and chant praise.
⁹Awake, O my soul; awake, lyre and harp!
I will wake the dawn.
¹⁰I will give thanks to you among the peoples, O Lord,
I will chant your praise among the nations,
¹¹For your kindness towers to the heavens,
and your faithfulness to the skies.
¹² Be exalted above the heavens, O God;
above all the earth be your glory!

(v. 9). No enemy can stand in the way of their joyous duty to give thanks publicly, by vows and offerings, for the life that God has given back to them.

Psalm 57

A lament (A) in which the victim of hostile actions by enemies (vv. 4, 5, 7) prays that God be a refuge and a protection. The drama of the lament, featuring the victim, the wicked, and God, is here especially vivid. The enemies are lions with teeth like swords to devour the just (v. 5); they dig a trap (v. 7). The psalmist expresses with deep feeling his fragility and his confidence in God's protecting presence. "The shadow of your wings" (v. 2) probably refers to the wings of the cherubim (powerful winged animals) whose wings spread over the ark, the throne of the invisible Lord, in the inner chamber of the temple (see 1 Kgs 6:23-28). The refrain "Be exalted . . . O God," is repeated boldly in verses 6 and 12. The psalmist's confession, "My heart is steadfast, O God" (vv. 8-11), is exceptionally vibrant and joyous. The whole psalm is the record of a sensitive yet exuberantly trustful person.

Psalm 58

In this lament (A) the psalmist expresses great trust in the Lord's power to dethrone all that stands in the way of the divine governance of the world.

PSALM 58

Against Unjust Judges

¹For the leader. (Do not destroy!) A *miktam* of David.

I

²Do you indeed like gods pronounce justice

and judge fairly, you men of rank?

³Nay, you willingly commit crimes;

on earth you look to the fruits of extortion.

⁴From the womb the wicked are perverted;

astray from birth have the liars gone.

⁵Theirs is poison like a serpent's,

like that of a stubborn snake that stops its ears,

⁶That it may not hear the voice of enchanters

casting cunning spells.

II

⁷O God, smash their teeth in their mouths;

the jaw-teeth of the lions, break, O Lord!

⁸Let them vanish like water flowing off;

when they draw the bow, let their arrows be headless shafts.

⁹Let them dissolve like a melting snail,

like an untimely birth that never sees the sun.

¹⁰Unexpectedly, like a thorn-bush,

or like thistles, let the whirlwind carry them away.

¹¹The just man shall be glad when he sees vengeance;

he shall bathe his feet in the blood of the wicked.

¹²And men shall say, "Truly there is a reward for the just;

truly there is a God who is judge on earth!"

PSALM 59

Against Bloodthirsty Enemies

¹For the leader. (Do not destroy!) A *miktam* of David when Saul sent men to watch his house and put him to death.

I

²Rescue me from my enemies, O my God;

from my adversaries defend me.

³Rescue me from evildoers;

from bloodthirsty men save me.

⁴For behold, they lie in wait for my life;

mighty men come together against me.

Not for any offense or sin of mine, O Lord;

⁵ for no guilt of mine they hurry to take up arms.

Rouse yourself to see it, and aid me,

⁶ for you are the Lord of hosts, the God of Israel.

Arise; punish all the nations;

have no pity on any worthless traitors.

The first verses condemn "the gods," the demonic forces that were popularly imagined to control human destinies (vv. 2-3), and "the wicked," the human instruments of these forces (vv. 4-6). Verses 7-12 pray that God take away their ability to harm the just (vv. 7-10). Such divine vengeance will make the righteous glad; they will see that their Lord is not indifferent to their suffering and has in fact upheld them.

Psalm 59

A lament (A) in which a person endangered by the lying tongues of those who seek to separate him from his God (vv. 7-8, 13, 15) prays that God will

7 Each evening they return, they
snarl like dogs
and prowl about the city.
8Though they bay with their mouths,
and blasphemies are on their lips—
"Who is there to listen?"—
9You, O LORD, laugh at them;
you deride all the nations.
10 O my strength! for you I watch;
for you, O God, are my stronghold,
11 my gracious God!

II
May God come to my aid;
may he show me the fall of my foes.
12O God, slay them, lest they beguile my
people;
shake them by your power, and bring
them down,
O Lord our shield!
13By the sin of their mouths and the word
of their lips
let them be caught in their arrogance,
for the lies they have told under oath.
14Consume them in wrath; consume, till
they are no more;
that men may know that God is the
ruler of Jacob,
yes, to the ends of the earth.
15 Each evening they return, they
snarl like dogs
and prowl about the city;

16They wander about as scavengers;
if they are not filled, they howl.
17But I will sing of your strength
and revel at dawn in your kindness;
You have been my stronghold,
my refuge in the day of distress.
18 O my strength! your praise will I
sing;
for you, O God, are my stronghold,
my gracious God!

PSALM 60

Prayer after Defeat in Battle

1For the leader; according to "The Lily of . . ." A
miktam of David (for teaching) 2when he fought
against Aram Naharaim and Aramzobah; and Joab,
coming back, killed twelve thousand Edomites in the
"valley of salt."

I
3O God, you have rejected us and broken our defenses;
you have been angry; rally us!
4You have rocked the country and split
it open;
repair the cracks in it, for it is tot-
tering.
5You have made your people feel hard-
ships;
you have given us stupefying wine.
6You have raised for those who fear you
a banner
to which they may flee out of bow-
shot

uphold him and punish them, and hence be seen as the just God of Israel. Verses 2-8 alternate prayer (vv. 2-3, 5b-6) and depictions of the wicked rampaging against the innocent psalmist (vv. 4-5a, 7-8). The psalmist vividly expresses confidence in the God who is just and loving (vv. 9-11). The near curse upon the enemies in verses 12-13 is not a crude desire for blood vengeance but a wish that the supremacy of Yahweh, about to break into human history, be recognized as such by all people (v. 14b). The God who rules the world (vv. 9, 14b) is also the God who rules the psalmist's life (vv. 17-18).

Psalm 60

In this community lament (A) the people dramatize their situation as defeated and deprived of their God-given land. Informing their complaint

⁷That your loved ones may escape;
  help us by your right hand, and answer us!

II

⁸God promised in his sanctuary:
  "Exultantly I will apportion Shechem,
  and measure off the valley of Suc-
  coth.
⁹Mine is Gilead, and mine Manasseh;
  Ephraim is the helmet for my head;
    Judah, my scepter;
¹⁰Moab shall serve as my washbowl;
  upon Edom I will set my shoe;
  I will triumph over Philistia."

III

¹¹Who will bring me into the fortified
    city?
  Who will lead me into Edom?
¹²Have not you, O God, rejected us,
  so that you go not forth, O God,
    with our armies?

¹³Give us aid against the foe,
  for worthless is the help of men.
¹⁴Under God we shall do valiantly;
  it is he who will tread down our foes.

PSALM 61
Prayer of the King in Exile

¹For the leader; with stringed instruments. Of
David.

I

²Hear, O God, my cry;
  listen to my prayer!
³From the earth's end I call to you
  as my heart grows faint.
  You will set me high upon a rock; you
    will give me rest,
⁴ for you are my refuge,
  a tower of strength against the
    enemy.
⁵Oh, that I might lodge in your tent
    forever,

before God is their conviction that they are "[God's] people," "those who fear [God]," "[God's] loved ones" (plural; vv. 5-7). They claim the protection of their God Yahweh, who is the Lord of all the nations of the earth. Yahweh has permitted their present plight and hence can reverse it.

The prayer of verse 7 is for an oracle of salvation; "answer us" is a special term for the seeking of the divine word of assurance in crises of war (see, for example, 1 Sam 14:37; 28:6, 15). The oracle of verses 8-10 is the divine response to the prayer, spoken by a priest in the temple. The Divine Warrior, through the priest, declares ownership of the land; the invasion of other nations is not permanent and will ultimately be reversed.

The territories mentioned in verses 8-9 were all part of the God-given territory. Whenever any were taken by an enemy, the people could hold God to that ancient oracle of grant. Verse 11 is the community's faith-response: "The land is ours; let's take it!" Verses 12-14 continue the opening lament, but now, in the light of the favorable divine promise, the words are uttered with a new confidence in the Lord and with a sober awareness of the limits of unaided human power.

Psalm 61

This psalmist, using elements of the lament (A) and thanksgiving form (B), prays in a place far distant from God's saving presence ("from the earth's

take refuge in the shelter of your
wings!

II

⁶You indeed, O God, have accepted my
vows;

you granted me the heritage of those
who fear your name.

⁷Add to the days of the king's life;
let his years be many generations;

⁸Let him sit enthroned before God
forever;

bid kindness and faithfulness preserve him.

⁹So will I sing the praises of your name
forever,

fulfilling my vows day by day.

PSALM 62

Trust in God Alone

¹For the leader; *'al Jeduthun.* A psalm of David.

I

² Only in God is my soul at rest;
from him comes my salvation.

³ He only is my rock and my salvation,

my stronghold; I shall not be
disturbed at all.

⁴How long will you set upon a man and
all together beat him down

as though he were a sagging fence, a
battered wall?

⁵Truly from my place on high they
plan to dislodge me;

they delight in lies;
They bless with their mouths,

but inwardly they curse.

II

⁶ Only in God be at rest, my soul,
for from him comes my hope.

⁷ He only is my rock and my salvation,

my stronghold; I shall not be
disturbed.

⁸With God is my safety and my glory,
he is the rock of my strength; my
refuge is in God.

⁹Trust in him at all times, O my people!
Pour out your hearts before him;
God is our refuge!

III

¹⁰Only a breath are mortal men;
an illusion are men of rank;

In a balance they prove lighter,
all together, than a breath.

end," v. 3) to be led to the security of God's presence. The language for security with God is traditional: rock, refuge, tower (vv. 3-5); to dwell forever
in the Lord's tent (see Pss 15:1; 27:4); beneath the outstretched wings of the
cherubim.

In the second half of the poem the psalmist confesses that God has come
to the rescue and given "the heritage [the land] of those who fear [God's]
name" to the one who trusted (v. 6). The holy land has a king; prayer is
offered that the king reflect adequately the divine vitality (vv. 7-8). The one
rescued is happy to sing praises to the name.

Psalm 62

This song of trust takes from the lament a sense of the fragility and danger
of life, and from the thanksgiving a serenity arising from the experience of
God's power. The serenity appears in the two refrains, verses 2-3 and 6-7,
with verse 8 expanding the theme; the anguish is in the angry taunt against
the rampaging wicked in verses 4-5. In verses 9-10 the psalmist steps for-

¹¹Trust not in extortion; in plunder take
   no empty pride;
   though wealth abound, set not your
      heart upon it.
¹²One thing God said; these two things
      which I heard:
   that power belongs to God, ¹³and
      yours, O Lord, is kindness;
   and that you render to everyone ac-
      cording to his deeds.

PSALM 63
Ardent Longing for God

¹A psalm of David, when he was in the wilderness
of Judah.

I

²O God, you are my God whom I seek;
   for you my flesh pines and my soul
      thirsts
   like the earth, parched, lifeless and
      without water.
³Thus have I gazed toward you in the
      sanctuary
   to see your power and your glory,
⁴For your kindness is a greater good
      than life;
   my lips shall glorify you.

II

⁵Thus will I bless you while I live;

lifting up my hands, I will call upon
      your name.
⁶As with the riches of a banquet shall
      my soul be satisfied,
   and with exultant lips my mouth
      shall praise you.
⁷I will remember you upon my couch,
   and through the night-watches I will
      meditate on you:
⁸That you are my help,
   and in the shadow of your wings I
      shout for joy.
⁹My soul clings fast to you;
   your right hand upholds me.

III

¹⁰But they shall be destroyed who seek
      my life,
   they shall go into the depths of the
      earth;
¹¹They shall be delivered over to the
      sword,
   and shall be the prey of jackals.

¹²The king, however, shall rejoice in
      God;
   everyone who swears by him shall
      glory,
   but the mouths of those who speak
      falsely shall be stopped.

ward as teacher to the community, so vivid has been his experience of God's power. That experience can be Israel's. Verse 12 reveals the astonishing source of the psalmist's contagious trust and inner poise: not the removal of danger but the word of God received as such, which relativizes all other powers.

Psalm 63

Like Psalm 61, this psalm also has elements of a lament (vv. 3-4 and 10-11), of a thanksgiving (vv. 4-6), and of a song of trust (vv. 7-9). The psalmist's situation explains the unusual juxtaposition of diverse genres: the psalmist, beset by liars and enemies (vv. 10, 12b), seeks God (v. 2) in the temple as an asylum in danger (vv. 3 and 8). He may even be spending the night in the sanctuary (vv. 7-8), intending to provoke a dream of reassurance. The one endangered then goes to the place of God's holy presence, the temple, in whose protective power he may be safe and where he can pray that justice be meted out to the wicked.

PSALM 64

Treacherous Conspirators Punished by God

¹For the leader. A psalm of David.

I

²Hear, O God, my voice in my lament;
  from the dread enemy preserve my life.
³Shelter me against the council of malefactors,
  against the tumult of evildoers,
⁴Who sharpen their tongues like swords,
  who aim like arrows their bitter words,
⁵Shooting from ambush at the innocent man,
  suddenly shooting at him without fear.
⁶They resolve on their wicked plan;
  they conspire to set snares,
  saying, "Who will see us?"
⁷They devise a wicked scheme,
  and conceal the scheme they have devised;
  deep are the thoughts of each heart.

II

⁸But God shoots his arrows at them;
  suddenly they are struck.
⁹He brings them down by their own tongues;
  all who see them nod their heads.
¹⁰And all men fear and proclaim the work of God,
  and ponder what he has done.
¹¹The just man is glad in the LORD and takes refuge in him;
  in him glory all the upright of heart.

PSALM 65

Thanksgiving for God's Blessings

¹For the leader. A psalm of David. A song.

I

²To you we owe our hymn of praise,
  O God, in Zion;
To you must vows be fulfilled,
  you who hear prayers.
³To you all flesh must come
⁴ because of wicked deeds.
We are overcome by our sins;
  it is you who pardon them.
⁵Happy the man you choose, and bring to dwell in your courts.
May we be filled with the good things of your house,
  the holy things of your temple!

Psalm 64

This lament (A) is uttered by a person who feels overwhelmed by the malice of the wicked, the enemies of the righteous in the psalms (vv. 2-7). They seek to cut off the individual from the holy people. Hence the prayer to destroy the evildoers' plan is vehement—that God turn against them the very arrows they had aimed against God's friends. The world will then see who is the true ruler of the world (vv. 8-10). Verse 11 is a vow of praise expressing the lively hope that God will bring about a just world.

Psalm 65

There are hymnic elements in this community thanksgiving (B), recited, most probably, at the festival when Israel enjoyed the fruits of the land. The festival could have been Pentecost, when wheat was harvested, or the feast of Ingathering of fruits, grapes, and olives in early autumn, when the rains resumed after the summer dry spell (vv. 10-14).

II

⁶With awe-inspiring deeds of justice you
    answer us,
    O God our savior,
The hope of all the ends of the earth
    and of the distant seas.
⁷You set the mountains in place by your
    power,
    you who are girt with might;
⁸You still the roaring of the seas,
    the roaring of their waves and the
    tumult of the peoples.
⁹And the dwellers at the earth's ends are
    in fear at your marvels;
    the farthest east and west you make
    resound with joy.

III

¹⁰You have visited the land and watered
    it;
    greatly have you enriched it.
God's watercourses are filled;
    you have prepared the grain.
¹¹Thus have you prepared the land:
    drenching its furrows,
    breaking up its clods,
Softening it with showers,
    blessing its yield.
¹²You have crowned the year with your
    bounty,
    and your paths overflow with a rich
    harvest;

¹³The untilled meadows overflow with it,
    and rejoicing clothes the hills.
¹⁴The fields are garmented with flocks
    and the valleys blanketed with grain.
    They shout and sing for joy.

PSALM 66

Praise of God, Israel's Deliverer

¹For the leader. A psalm; a song.

Shout joyfully to God, all you on earth,
² sing praise to the glory of his name;
    proclaim his glorious praise.
³Say to God, "How tremendous are your
    deeds!
    for your great strength your enemies
    fawn upon you.
⁴Let all on earth worship and sing praise
    to you,
    sing praise to your name!"

I

⁵Come and see the works of God,
    his tremendous deeds among men.
⁶He has changed the sea into dry land;
    through the river they passed on
    foot;
    therefore let us rejoice in him.
⁷He rules by his might forever;
    his eyes watch the nations;
    rebels may not exalt themselves.
⁸Bless our God, you peoples,

The Lord is given praise for three mercies: for making Zion a place of encounter and reconciliation for the holy people (vv. 2-5); for overcoming the primordial unbounded waters that once covered the earth and prevented human life from appearing (vv. 6-9); and for making those same waters fertilize the earth to bear fruit (vv. 10-14).

Psalm 66

In genre, this liturgical poem resembles a hymn (C) in verses 1-12 and an individual thanksgiving (B) in verses 13-20; it is now a unified liturgy. Verses 1-2 contain an invitatory exhorting the world to acknowledge Israel's God as uniquely powerful. The greatest proof of this power is the way Yahweh broke the sea's power to keep Israel from its land; let the nations revere this just God (vv. 5-7). Israel's history, the story of its humiliation and exaltation (probably the Babylonian Exile and the restoration), witnesses to God's

loudly sound his praise;
⁹He has given life to our souls,
and has not let our feet slip.
¹⁰For you have tested us, O God!
You have tried us as silver is tried by fire;
¹¹You have brought us into a snare;
you laid a heavy burden on our backs.
¹²You let men ride over our heads;
we went through fire and water,
but you have led us out to refreshment.

II

¹³I will bring holocausts to your house;
to you I will fulfill the vows
¹⁴Which my lips uttered
and my words promised in my distress.
¹⁵Holocausts of fatlings I will offer you,
with burnt offerings of rams;
I will sacrifice oxen and goats.
¹⁶Hear now, all you who fear God, while I declare
what he has done for me.
¹⁷When I appealed to him in words,
praise was on the tip of my tongue.
¹⁸Were I to cherish wickedness in my heart,
the LORD would not hear;

¹⁹But God has heard;
he has hearkened to the sound of my prayer.
²⁰Blessed be God who refused me not
my prayer or his kindness!

PSALM 67

Harvest Prayer That All Men May Worship God

¹For the leader; with stringed instruments. A psalm; a song.

I

²May God have pity on us and bless us;
may he let his face shine upon us.
³So may your way be known upon earth;
among all nations, your salvation.
⁴   May the peoples praise you, O God;
    may all the peoples praise you!

II

⁵May the nations be glad and exult
because you rule the peoples in equity;
the nations on the earth you guide.
⁶   May the peoples praise you, O God;

justice and fidelity—justice, because God punished Israel's sins; fidelity, because God did not abandon the people forever (vv. 8-12).

Any member of this sinful yet rescued people may acknowledge the merciful God through appropriate sacrifice (vv. 13-16). As often in thanksgiving, the one who has experienced God's mercy steps forward as teacher; God is ready to be merciful to all who repent (vv. 16-20).

Psalm 67

The psalm reflects a temple liturgy in which the congregation echoes a part of the famous benediction of Aaron (Num 6:24-26). The people affirm the priestly blessing (v. 2), conscious that their God-given prosperity witnesses to the mercy and power of their God (v. 3). The first of two refrains, inviting the nations to acknowledge Yahweh (v. 4), serves as preface to the statement that Yahweh guides the nations; the second refrain (v. 6) serves as preface to the statement that Yahweh makes the earth bountiful.

may all the peoples praise
you!

III

⁷The earth has yielded its fruits;
God, our God, has blessed us.
⁸May God bless us,
and may all the ends of the earth
fear him!

PSALM 68

God's Triumphal Procession

¹For the leader. A psalm of David; a song.

I

²God arises; his enemies are scattered,
and those who hate him flee before
him.
³As smoke is driven away, so are they
driven;
as wax melts before the fire,
so the wicked perish before God.
⁴But the just rejoice and exult before
God;
they are glad and rejoice.

II

⁵Sing to God, chant praise to his name,
extol him who rides upon the
clouds,
Whose name is the Lᴏʀᴅ;
exult before him.
⁶The father of orphans and the defender
of widows
is God in his holy dwelling.
⁷God gives a home to the forsaken;
he leads forth prisoners to prosperity;
only rebels remain in the parched
land.

III

⁸O God, when you went forth at the
head of your people,

when you marched through the
wilderness,
⁹The earth quaked; it rained from heaven
at the presence of God,
at the presence of God, the God of
Israel, the One of Sinai.
¹⁰A bountiful rain you showered down,
O God, upon your inheritance;
you restored the land when it lan-
guished;
¹¹Your flock settled in it;
in your goodness, O God, you pro-
vided it for the needy.

IV

¹²The Lord gives the word;
women bear the glad tidings, a vast
army:
¹³"Kings and their hosts are fleeing, fleeing,
and the household shall divide the
spoils.
¹⁴Though you rested among the sheep-
folds,
the wings of the dove shone with
silver,
and her pinions with a golden hue.
¹⁵While the Almighty dispersed the kings
there,
snow fell on Zalmon."

V

¹⁶High the mountains of Bashan;
rugged the mountains of Bashan.
¹⁷Why look you jealously, you rugged
mountains,
at the mountain God has chosen for
his throne,
where the Lᴏʀᴅ himself will dwell
forever?
¹⁸The chariots of God are myriad, thousands on thousands;

Psalm 68

About no other psalm are there so many and such radically different in-
terpretations. The text is disturbed. Some scholars believe that the psalm is
simply a collection of short fragments. This commentary sees the psalm as
reflecting a liturgical ceremony, a procession to the temple; it is like Pss 24;
106:19-29; and 2 Sam 6.

the Lord advances from Sinai to the sanctuary.
¹⁹You have ascended on high, taken captives,
received men as gifts—
even rebels; the LORD God enters his dwelling.

VI
²⁰Blessed day by day be the Lord,
who bears our burdens; God, who is our salvation.
²¹God is a saving God for us;
the LORD, my Lord, controls the passageways of death.
²²Surely God crushes the heads of his enemies,
the hairy crowns of those who stalk about in their guilt.
²³The Lord said: "I will fetch them back from Bashan;
I will fetch them back from the depths of the sea,
²⁴So that you will bathe your feet in blood;
the tongues of your dogs will have their share of your enemies."

VII
²⁵They view your progress, O God,
the progress of my God, my King, into the sanctuary;
²⁶The singers lead, the minstrels follow,
in their midst the maidens play on timbrels.

²⁷In your choirs bless God;
bless the Lord, you of Israel's well-spring!
²⁸There is Benjamin, the youngest, leading them;
the princes of Judah in a body,
the princes of Zebulun, the princes of Naphtali.

VIII
²⁹Show forth, O God, your power,
the power, O God, with which you took our part;
³⁰For your temple in Jerusalem
let the kings bring you gifts.
³¹Rebuke the wild beast of the reeds,
the herd of strong bulls and the bullocks, the nations.
Let them prostrate themselves with bars of silver;
scatter the peoples who delight in war.
³²Let nobles come from Egypt;
let Ethiopia extend its hands to God.

IX
³³You kingdoms of the earth, sing to God,
chant praise to the Lord
³⁴ who rides on the heights of the ancient heavens.
Behold, his voice resounds, the voice of power:
³⁵ "Confess the power of God!"
Over Israel is his majesty;

In verses 2-7 the procession begins, the people following the ark of the covenant, the throne upon which Yahweh is invisibly enthroned. The movement of so powerful a Deity frightens any possible foes but gladdens friends. In verses 8-21 the procession of the ark symbolizes the great battle between Yahweh and Yahweh's enemies, Sea or Death. The evil powers were defeated, and a shrine to the victory was prepared (vv. 16-19). The psalmist acknowledges that the victory of Yahweh over the forces of chaos creates a just world in which the righteous will be safe from the attacks of the wicked (vv. 20-24). The procession includes all the tribes of Israel, rejoicing in their unity (vv. 25-28). The psalm ends with a warning to the nations: recognize the one God and honor God's people.

his power is in the skies.
³⁶Awesome in his sanctuary is God, the God of Israel;
he gives power and strength to his people.
Blessed be God!

PSALM 69

A Cry of Anguish in Great Distress

¹For the leader; according to "Lilies." Of David.

I

²Save me, O God,
for the waters threaten my life;
³I am sunk in the abysmal swamp
where there is no foothold;
I have reached the watery depths;
the flood overwhelms me.
⁴I am wearied with calling,
my throat is parched;
My eyes have failed
with looking for my God.
⁵Those outnumber the hairs of my head
who hate me without cause.
Too many for my strength
are they who wrongfully are my enemies.
Must I restore what I did not steal?

II

⁶O God, you know my folly,
and my faults are not hid from you.
⁷Let not those who wait for you be put to shame through me,
O Lord, GOD of hosts.
Let not those who seek you blush for me,
O God of Israel,
⁸Since for your sake I bear insult,
and shame covers my face.
⁹I have become an outcast to my brothers,
a stranger to my mother's sons,
¹⁰Because zeal for your house consumes me,
and the insults of those who blaspheme you fall upon me.
¹¹I humbled myself with fasting,
and this was made a reproach to me.
¹²I made sackcloth my garment,
and I became a byword for them.
¹³They who sit at the gate gossip about me,
and drunkards make me the butt of their songs.

III

¹⁴But I pray to you, O LORD,
for the time of your favor, O God!
In your great kindness answer me
with your constant help.
¹⁵Rescue me out of the mire; may I not sink!
may I be rescued from my foes,
and from the watery depths.
¹⁶Let not the flood-waters overwhelm me,
nor the abyss swallow me up,
nor the pit close its mouth over me.
¹⁷Answer me, O LORD, for bounteous is your kindness;
in your great mercy turn toward me.
¹⁸Hide not your face from your servant;
in my distress, make haste to answer me.

Psalm 69

The psalm is a lament (A), unusual by its length and by the sufferer's keen sense of suffering for the Lord (vv. 8, 11-12). The depiction of suffering is both metaphorical (vv. 2-3; 15-16: the waters characterize chaos before God creates) and realistic (vv. 4, 5, 9, 11-13: exhaustion, alienation from family and community, misunderstanding of religious acts). Especially in the second part of the psalm is there fervent prayer that the enemies be punished (vv. 23-29). God's punishment of the psalmist's enemies is public vindication of the psalmist. As in other laments, the psalmist expresses hope

¹⁹Come and ransom my life;
  as an answer for my enemies, redeem
  me.
²⁰You know my reproach, my shame and
  my ignominy:
  before you are all my foes.
²¹Insult has broken my heart, and I am
  weak,
  I looked for sympathy, but there
  was none;
  for comforters, and I found none.
²²Rather they put gall in my food,
  and in my thirst they gave me vine-
  gar to drink.

IV
²³Let their own table be a snare before
  them,
  and a net for their friends.
²⁴Let their eyes grow dim so that they
  cannot see,
  and keep their backs always feeble.
²⁵Pour out your wrath upon them;
  let the fury of your anger overtake
  them.
²⁶Let their encampment become deso-
  late;
  in their tents let there be no one to
  dwell.
²⁷For they kept after him whom you
  smote,
  and added to the pain of him you
  wounded.
²⁸Heap guilt upon their guilt,
  and let them not attain to your reward.
²⁹May they be erased from the book of
  the living,
  and not be recorded with the just!

V
³⁰But I am afflicted and in pain;
  let your saving help, O God, protect
  me.
³¹I will praise the name of God in song,
  and I will glorify him with thanksgiving;
³²This will please the LORD more than
  oxen
  or bullocks with horns and divided
  hooves:
³³"See, you lowly ones, and be glad;
  you who seek God, may your hearts
  be merry!
³⁴For the LORD hears the poor,
  and his own who are in bonds he
  spurns not.
³⁵Let the heavens and the earth praise
  him,
  the seas and whatever moves in
  them!"
³⁶For God will save Zion
  and rebuild the cities of Judah.
  They shall dwell in the land and own it,
³⁷ and the descendants of his servants
  shall inherit it,
  and those who love his name shall
  inhabit it.

PSALM 70
Prayer for Divine Help

¹For the leader; of David. For remembrance.
²Deign, O God, to rescue me;
  O LORD, make haste to help me.
³Let them be put to shame and confounded
  who seek my life.

in God and makes a vow of praise at the end (vv. 31-37); the vow recognizes
that God is more pleased with praise than with sacrifice. The sufferer fasts
and laments, conscious of the need for purification before the all-holy God,
who is no longer encountered in the destroyed temple. These gestures are
misinterpreted by his enemies, who judge him to be guilty and rightly afflicted by God. The psalmist's situation of suffering for the Lord and his hope
of vindication by an attentive and faithful God applies to all servants of the
Lord (vv. 18, 36-37).

Let them be turned back in disgrace
  who desire my ruin.
[4]Let them retire in their shame
  who say to me, "Aha, aha!"
[5]But may all who seek you
  exult and be glad in you,
And may those who love your salvation
  say ever, "God be glorified!"
[6]But I am afflicted and poor;
  O God, hasten to me!
You are my help and my deliverer;
  O LORD, hold not back!

PSALM 71

Humble Prayer in Time of Old Age

I

[1]In you, O LORD, I take refuge;
  let me never be put to shame.
[2]In your justice rescue me, and deliver
  me;
  incline your ear to me, and save me.
[3]Be my rock of refuge,
  a stronghold to give me safety,
  for you are my rock and my fortress.
[4]O my God, rescue me from the hand of
  the wicked,
  from the grasp of the criminal and the
  violent.
[5]For you are my hope, O Lord;
  my trust, O God, from my youth.
[6]On you I depend from birth;

from my mother's womb you are my
  strength;
  constant has been my hope in you.
[7]A portent am I to many,
  but you are my strong refuge!
[8]My mouth shall be filled with your
  praise,
  with your glory day by day.

II

[9]Cast me not off in my old age;
  as my strength fails, forsake me not,
[10]For my enemies speak against me,
  and they who keep watch against my
  life take counsel together.
[11]They say, "God has forsaken him;
  pursue and seize him,
  for there is no one to rescue him."
[12]O God, be not far from me;
  my God, make haste to help me.
[13]Let them be put to shame and consumed who attack my life;
  let them be wrapped in ignominy and
  disgrace who seek to harm me.
[14]But I will always hope
  and praise you ever more and more.
[15]My mouth shall declare your justice,
  day by day your salvation,
  though I know not their extent.
[16]I will treat of the mighty works of the
  LORD;
  O God, I will tell of your singular
  justice.

Psalm 70

In this lament (A) one of the "afflicted and poor" (v. 6), a group which recognizes that they have no other resource than Yahweh, cries out to be saved from the enemy, "who seek my life" (v. 3). May the group of righteous, to which the psalmist belongs, be upheld with the divine presence that brings joy to the heart (vv. 5-6)!

Psalm 71

This lament (A) is uttered by an old person (v. 9) who seeks asylum in the temple. Persecuted by enemies, who interpret the afflictions of old age as divine judgment (v. 11), the psalmist turns to the God of righteousness whose praise he has sung from his youth. Verses 1-4 are an impassioned cry to God, the immovable rock of refuge. Verses 5-9 express a hope learned

III

¹⁷O God, you have taught me from my
youth,
  and till the present I proclaim your
  wondrous deeds;
¹⁸And now that I am old and gray,
  O God, forsake me not
Till I proclaim your strength
  to every generation that is to come.
¹⁹Your power and your justice,
  O God, reach to heaven.
You have done great things;
  O God, who is like you?
²⁰Though you have made me feel many
  bitter afflictions,
  you will again revive me;
  from the depths of the earth you will
  once more raise me.
²¹Renew your benefits toward me,
  and comfort me over and over.
²²So will I give you thanks with music
  on the lyre,
  for your faithfulness, O my God!
I will sing your praises with the harp,
  O Holy One of Israel!
²³My lips shall shout for joy
  as I sing your praises;
My soul also, which you have re-
  deemed,
²⁴ and my tongue day by day shall discourse on your justice.
How shamed and how disgraced
  are those who sought to harm me!

PSALM 72

The Kingdom of the Messiah

¹Of Solomon.

I

O God, with your judgment endow the
king,
  and with your justice, the king's son;
²He shall govern your people with justice
  and your afflicted ones with judgment.
³The mountains shall yield peace for
  the people,
  and the hills justice.
⁴He shall defend the afflicted among the
  people,
  save the children of the poor,
  and crush the oppressor.

II

⁵May he endure as long as the sun,
  and like the moon through all generations.
⁶He shall be like rain coming down on
  the meadow,
  like showers watering the earth.
⁷Justice shall flower in his days,
  and profound peace, till the moon be
  no more.

III

⁸May he rule from sea to sea,
  and from the River to the ends of the
  earth.

from a lifetime of praising God. Verses 10-13 dramatize the menace of the
enemies and pray for their downfall. Verses 14-21 develop a prayer for deliverance. The psalmist has sung of God's wonders all these years. Will God allow
that voice of praise to grow silent under the attack of enemies? Verses 22-24
are a vow of praise; the psalmist, in the light of the reassuring oracle given
by the priest in the temple, will continue the song of praise begun in his youth.

Psalm 72

This royal psalm presents the king as the vicar of Yahweh. He represents
to Israel and to the world the justice and peace with which the world was
created. The king, however, is a human being who gives only what he has
been given; intercession must be made for him. Intercession is the purpose
of the psalm.

⁹His foes shall bow before him,
and his enemies shall lick the dust.
¹⁰The kings of Tarshish and the Isles shall
offer gifts;
the kings of Arabia and Seba shall
bring tribute.
¹¹All kings shall pay him homage,
all nations shall serve him.

IV

¹²For he shall rescue the poor man when
he cries out,
and the afflicted when he has no one
to help him.
¹³He shall have pity for the lowly and the
poor;
the lives of the poor he shall save.
¹⁴From fraud and violence he shall redeem them,
and precious shall their blood be in
his sight.

V

¹⁵May he live to be given the gold of
Arabia,
and to be prayed for continually;

day by day shall they bless him.
¹⁶May there be an abundance of grain
upon the earth;
on the tops of the mountains the
crops shall rustle like Lebanon;
the city dwellers shall flourish like
the verdure of the fields.
¹⁷May his name be blessed forever;
as long as the sun his name shall remain.
In him shall all the tribes of the earth
be blessed;
all the nations shall proclaim his hap-
piness.

*   *   *

¹⁸Blessed be the LORD, the God of
Israel,
who alone does wondrous deeds.
¹⁹And blessed forever be his glorious
name;
may the whole earth be filled with
his glory.
Amen. Amen.
²⁰The prayers of David the son of Jesse
are ended.

In verses 1-4, echoed in verses 12-14, the king is the "lengthened arm of Yahweh," exercising divine judgment. Justice here—and generally in the Bible—is not impartial deciding but vigorous upholding of the oppressed party. Verses 12-14 state that the king redeems the life of the poor; he is the agent of Yahweh's rescue of the people. The king embodies not only divine justice but also divinely intended peace and fertility; in verses 5-7 and 16 he embodies health and fertility for the whole land. Yahweh, the sole Deity in heaven and on earth, has a sole vicar, the Israelite king. To that king, therefore, all the nations of the earth come, bringing gifts that acknowledge the just and life-giving divine presence manifest in him (vv. 17-19).

REVIEW AIDS AND DISCUSSION TOPICS

I

Introduction (pages 5–7)

1. What is at the center of every psalm? What is the most common way in which the psalms conceive the presence of God? In what activity in the temple was that presence most real?

2. What other modes of presence did the psalmists believe served to reveal God to Israel? Give examples of psalms that show God to be present in the king and in the word or the law.

3. What is the basis for the Christian use of the psalms? In what way is Christ the new temple, the king, the word?

4. How does the lament resemble a drama? Why do scholars assume that a word of assurance is given to the petitioner in every lament?

5. What is the essence of a thanksgiving? How do the psalms in general say "thank you" to God?

6. What is the basis for praise in the hymn?

7. What effect upon psalm interpretation is made by the superscription about David?

II

Book I: Psalms 1–41 (pages 8–47)

1. *Psalm 1.* What are the "two ways" open to every person? How do punishment and reward come about in this psalm? Do you find this way of conceiving your life helpful?

2. *Psalm 2.* Why is the Israelite king the ruler of the world in principle? How might this psalm be applied to Christ?

3. *Psalm 7.* Why can the psalmist claim to be an innocent just person? Why is there need of a *public* punishment of the enemies?

4. *Psalm 15.* Why must the Israelite be admitted to the temple court by the priest rather than enter it spontaneously? What other lists of ten or twelve stipulations can you think of in the Old Testament?

5. *Psalm 18.* Why is the king so important in this psalm? What purpose is served by having two parallel accounts of the rescue?

6. *Psalm 37.* What does the teacher of the psalm believe will happen in the future that will solve the people's problem? What echoes of this psalm do you find in the beatitudes of the New Testament (Matt 5:3-12 and Luke 6:20-26)?

III

Book II: Psalms 42–72 (pages 47–77)

1. *Psalms 42–43.* What do these psalms teach about the place where the Israelites believed God to be present? What does the phrase "Where is your God?" mean in Ps 42:11?

2. *Psalm 44.* What is the present situation that contrasts so sharply with the original glorious state? What does this psalm affirm about being the Lord's people in adversity?

3. *Psalm 48.* Why does this psalm give all the titles to Mount Zion (vv. 2-4)? Why are the very buildings so sacred (vv. 13-15)?

4. *Psalm 49.* What is the problem and the solution to the problem? Are you satisfied with the statement of both?

5. *Psalm 51.* Why has this psalm been so popular throughout the ages? How are sin and forgiveness understood in the psalm?

6. *Psalm 69.* What literary means does the psalmist use to communicate acute suffering? Why is the sufferer misunderstood by fellow Israelites? What is the reason for the prayer to punish the enemies?